CONTENTS

Introduction 9

Keto diet and weight loss 11

Top 6 Keto Tips 12

Introduction to Instant Pot 13

Great Tips for Using Your Instant Pot 14

INSTANT POT KETO POULTRY RECIPES 15

Healthy Marinara Chicken with Cauliflower Risotto 15

Buffalo Chicken Fingers with Nutty Kale Salad 16

Healthy Roasted Turkey with Low Carb Avocado Relish 16

Instant Pot Healthy Turkey Meat Balls 17

Delicious Turkey Sausage Patties with Lemon Tahini Sauce 17

Instant Pot Roast Chicken with Steamed Veggies 18

Healthy Chicken Curry 18

Low Carb Turkey Served with Creamy Sauce and Sautéed Capers 19

Tasty Instant Pot Thai Turkey Legs 19

Gingery Roasted Turkey 20

Herbed Instant Pot Turkey Breast 20

Tangy Instant Pot Turkey Meatballs 21

Pressure Roasted Chicken 21

Tasty Instant Pot Turkey Breast 22

Pressure Cooked Cajun Chicken with Lime Butter Steamed Veggies 22

Instant Pot Ginger Peach Chicken 23

Instant Pot Asian chicken lettuce wraps 23

Oregano Chicken with Sautéed Kale 24

Tasty Citric Chicken with Fried Button Mushrooms 24

Low Carb Turkey Ratatouille 25

Spiced Chicken Patties Low Carb Lemon Pesto 25

Vegetable & Chicken Stir-Fry 26

Turkey-Cauliflower Hash with Avocado and Hardboiled Egg 26

Instant Pot Chicken Curry 27

Healthy Turkey Loaf with Sautéed Button Mushrooms 27

Satisfying Turkey Lettuce Wraps 28

Lemon Olive Chicken 28

Instant Pot Turkey with Veggies 29

Instant Pot Baked Chicken with Salsa 29

Instant Pot Crunchy Chicken Salad 30

Pressure Cooked Chicken Shawarma 30

Instant Pot Coconut Curry Turkey 31

Instant Pot Green Chile Chicken 31

Healthy Chicken Super Salad 32

Grilled Herb Marinade Chicken with Sautéed Mushrooms 32

Tropical Turkey Salad 33

Instant Pot Grilled Chicken & Green Onion 33

Healthy Turkey Chili 34

INSTANT POT KETO EGG RECIPES 34

Breakfast Meaty Quiche 34

Breakfast Eggs de Provence 35

Instant Pot Keto Bacon-Spinach Frittata 35

Roasted Veggie Breakfast Frittata 36

Instant Pot Avocado Shrimp Omelet 36

Healthy Frittata w/ Scallions & Smoked Salmon 37

Instant Pot Cheesy Green Omelet 37

Instant Pot Sausage & Broccoli Quiche 38

Instant Pot Salmon Omelet 38

Low-Carb Keto Instant Pot Egg Salad 39

Instant Pot Keto Jalapeno Omelettes 39

Instant Pot Keto Mini Mushroom Quiche 40

Keto Breakfast Casserole 40

Healthy Veggie Frittata 41

Instant Pot Frittata with Pesto 41

Instant Pot Berry Omelet 42

Instant Pot Low Carb Casserole 42

Asian Breakfast Eggs 43

Keto Mexican Frittata 43

Low Carb Instant Pot Egg Cups 44

Instant Pot Spiced Salmon Frittata 44

Korean Steamed Breakfast Eggs 45

Pressure Cooked Zucchini & Beef Frittata 45

Instant Pot Breakfast Casserole 46

Easy Breakfast Casserole 46

Keto Mini Mushroom Quiche 47

Instant Pot Breakfast Eggs & Sausage 47

Green Eggs with Bacon 48

Instant Pot Egg Mug 48

Instant Pot Greek Breakfast Sausage 49

INSTANT POT VEGETARIAN AND VEGAN KETO RECIPES 50

Sage-Infused Butternut Squash Zucchini Noodles 50

Instant Pot Coconut Curry Tofu 51

Asian Saag Aloo 51

Creamy Cauliflower 'Mashed Potatoes' 52

Instant Pot Spanish Tortilla 52

Sage-Infused Butternut Squash Zucchini Noodles 53

Keto Coconut Porridge 53

Instant Pot Coconut Cabbage 54

Yummy Brussels Sprouts 54

Peperonata (Tasty Pepper Salad) 55

Instant Pot Korean Breakfast Eggs 55

Arugula, Orange & Kamut Salad 56

Creamy Cauliflower Mash 56

Delicious Sage-Infused Butternut Squash Zucchini Noodles 57

Tasty Coconut Cabbage 57

Instant Pot Freekeh & Roasted Cauliflower w/ Tahini Sauce 58

Yummy Refried Beans 59

Pressure Cooked Navy Beans, Split Pea & Sweet Potatoes Bowl 59

Healthy Italian Mushrooms 60

Instant Pot Low Carb Veggie Dish 60

Instant Pot Keto Ham & Greens 61

Mixed Veggie Pot Pie 61

Instant Pot Pepper Salad 62

Egg- Sauerkraut Salad 62

Broccoli & Cauliflower Mash 63

Cheese & Broccoli Casserole 63

Keto Gluten-Free Coconut Breakfast Cereal 64

Low Carb Oatmeal 64

Tasty Keto Spiced Pecans 65

Crusty Spinach Pie 65

INSTANT POT KETO SOUPS 66

Instant Pot Turkey & Coconut Soup 66

Instant Pot Detox Veggie Soup 66

Instant Pot Spicy Green Soup 67

Instant Pot Easy Everyday Chicken Soup 67

Comforting Chicken Soup w/ Avocado 68

Creamy Instant Pot Chicken & Tomato Soup 68

Instant Pot Flat-Belly Soup 69

Instant Pot Tomato Basil Soup 69

Instant Pot Seafood Soup 70

Tasty Mushroom Coconut Milk Soup 70

Tasty Mushroom Coconut Milk Soup 71

Instant Pot Detox Veggie Soup 71

Instant Pot Spicy Green Soup 72

Lemony Veggie Soup w/ Cayenne 72

Mushroom Coconut Soup 73

Instant Pot Black Bean Chipotle Soup 73

Instant Pot Spicy Coconut Cauliflower Soup 74

Farmhouse Veggie Soup 74

Hot Instant Pot Vegetable Soup 75

Chicken Enchilada Soup 75

Mushroom Coconut Soup 76

Instant Pot Spicy Green Soup 76

Yummy Minestrone Soup 77

Instant Pot French Onion Soup 77

Pressure Cooked Vegetable Soup 78

Healthy Keto Hot & Sour Soup 78

Creamy Chicken Soup with Sautéed Cauliflower Rice 79

Instant Pot Spiced Turkey Soup 79

Instant Pot Cream of Carrot Soup 80

Instant Pot Broccoli & Blue Cheese Soup 80

Italian Meatball Zoodle Soup 81

Instant Pot Indian Curried Vegetable Soup 81

Three- Ingredient Instant Pot Veggie Beef Soup 82

Low Carb Italian Gnocchi Soup 82

Instant Pot Keto Bolognese Mince Soup 83

Low Carb Curried Vegetable Soup 83

Smoky Pork Cassoulet Soup 84

South African Cabbage & Boerewors Soup 84

INSTANT POT KETO STEWS 85

Instant Pot Spiced Coconut Fish Stew 85

Instant Pot Chicken and Vegetable Stew 85

Ground Beef and Vegetable Stew 86

Instant Pot Spiced and Creamy Vegetable Stew with Cashews 86

Coconut Fish Stew with Spinach 87

Filling Herbed Turkey Stew 87

Low Carb Bouillabaisse Fish Stew 88

Instant Pot Thai Nut Chicken 88

Tasty Instant Pot Greek Fish Stew 89

Pressure Cooker Vegetable and Fish Stew 89

Easy Cheesy Turkey Stew 90

Instant Pot Beef and Sweet Potato Stew 90

Instant Pot Coconut Fish Stew 91

Instant Pot Loaded Protein Stew 91

Instant Pot Low Carb Mussel Stew 92

Scrumptious Beef Stew 92

Turkish Split Pea Stew 93

Delicious Seafood Stew 93

Curried Chicken Stew 94

Beef Chuck & Green Cabbage Stew 94

Madras Lamb Stew 95

Curried Goat Stew 95

Instant Pot Lemon Chicken Stew 96

Hearty Lamb & Cabbage Stew 96

Rosemary-Garlic Beef Stew 97

Instant Pot Oxtail Stew 97

Pressure Cooked Lamb-Bacon Stew 98

Instant Pot Low Carb Vegetable Stew 98

Best Beef Stew for a King! 99

INSTANT POT KETO BEEF RECIPES 99

Healthy Italian Beef & Cabbage Stir-Fry 99

Instant Pot Beef Shred Rolls serve with Chilled Lemon Juice 100

Delicious Instant Pot Steak with Parsley & Arugula 100

Filet Mignon with Caramelized Onions 101

Healthy Beef Chili served with Avocado and Green Onions 101

Ground Beef with Veggies 102

Herbed London Broil with Lemon Garlic Butter Zucchini Noodles 102

Low Carb Beef & Sweet Potato Dish 103

Asparagus & Steak Bowl 103

Crunchy Steak Salad 104

Mango Chili Beef Stir Fry 104

Creamy Beef, Red Pepper & Cucumber Salad 105

Instant Pot Lemon Beef Steak 105

Instant Pot Beef Curry 106

Steak Salad with Spiced Avocado Dressing 106

Healthy Zucchini Beef Sauté with Avocado 107

Low Carb Ground Beef Tacos with Salsa 107

Pepper Crusted Steak with Garlic Creamed Sautéed Spinach 108

Steak Frites with Rocket & Peppercorn Sauce 108

Lean Steak with Oregano-Orange Chimichurri & Arugula Salad 109

Instant Pot Paleo Meatballs 109

Beef and Zucchini Lasagna 110

Instant Pot Barbacoa 110

Pressure Cooked Italian Beef 111

Roast Red Wine Beef Steak with Chili Olive Salsa 112

Instant Pot Chipotle Shredded Beef 113

Instant Pot AIP Beef 113

Beef & Sweet Potato Enchilada Casserole 114

Instant Pot Beef Roast 114

Paleo Instant Pot Beef Jalapeno Chili 115

Low Carb Cheese Steak Casserole with Fresh Lemon Juice 115

Tasty Lime Steak with Green Salad 116

Loaded Low Carb Flank Steak with Steamed Asian Veggies 116

Beef Stir Fry with Red Onions & Cabbage 117

Chili Fried Steak with Toasted Cashews & Sautéed Spinach 117

Protein-Rich Beef & Veggie Stew 118

Peppered Steak with Cherry Tomatoes 118

Keto Ground Beef Chili served with Avocado 119

Loaded Flank Steak with Salsa 119

Instant Pot Beef & Zucchini 120

Coriander & Buttermilk Steak with Salad 120

Cheese Stuffed Meatloaf Stuffed 121

INSTANT POT KETO PORK RECIPES 121

Feta & Spinach Stuffed Pork 121

Pressure Cooked Sour Cream Pork Chops 122

Four-Ingredient Pork Chops 122

Instant Pot Low Lime Carb Pork Carnitas 123

Low Carb Pork Tenderloin 123

Pressure Cooked Parmesan Dijon Crusted Pork Chops 124

Instant Pot Pork Chops with Steamed Veggies & Creamy Sesame Dressing 125

Shredded Pressure-Cooked Pork with Green Salad and Avocado 126

Instant Pot Pork Chops with Bacon & Caramelized Onions 126

Instant Pot BBQ Pork Wraps 127

Pork & Mushroom Dumplings 127

Instant Pot Low Carb Spiced Pork Chops 128

Barbecued Pork Chops with Broccoli 128

Keto Bone-In Pork Chops 129

Pork Roast w/ Cauliflower Gravy 129

Italian Pulled Pork Ragu 130

Instant Pot Herbed Pork 130

Pressure Cooked Jamaican Jerk Pork Roast 131

Instant Pot Crisp Chinese pork with Yummy Broccoli Mash 131

Instant Pot Pork Salad 132

Instant Pot Citrus Pork 132

Instant Pot BBQ Pork Ribs 133

Ingredients 133

Directions 133

Instant Pot Spiced Pork Chops 133

Instant Pot Pork Chops 134

Lemon & Herb Pork Chops 134

Instant Pot Pork Rind Stuffed Peppers 135

Keto Instant Spiced Pork Chops 135

Instant Pot Cheese Crusted Pork Chops 136

Pork Chops in Cream Sauce served with Avocado 136

Caramelized Onion Pork Chops with Steamed Green Beans and Avocado 137

INSTANT POT KETO SEAFOOD AND FISH RECIPES 137

Instant Pot Coconut Fishbowl 137

Instant Pot Shrimp Paella 138

Steamed Alaskan Crab Legs 138

Instant Pot Shrimp & Grits 139

Salmon with Gingery Orange Sauce 140

Instant Pot Mussels 140

Salmon w/ Chili-Lime Sauce 141

Instant Pot Tilapia 141

Pressure Cooked Coconut Curry Shrimp 142

Hot Lemony Tilapia w/ Asparagus 142

Tasty Citrus Tilapia 143

Pressure Steamed Salmon 143

Teriyaki Fish w/ Zucchini 144

Grilled Tuna w/ Bean & Tomato Salad 144

Steamed Bass with Fennel, Parsley, and Capers 145

Pressure Baked Salmon Salad with Mint Dressing 145

Spiced Mahi-Mahi with Creamed Sautéed Mushrooms 146

Instant Pot Seafood Cioppino 146

Instant Pot Shrimp Scampi 147

Instant Pot BBQ Shrimp 147

Spicy Grilled Cod 148

Coconut Fish & Vegetable Curry 149

Red Snapper in Hot Veggie Sauce 149

Pressure Grilled Salmon 150

Creamy Coconut Baked Salmon with Green Salad 150

Tilapia with Mushroom Sauce 151

Pressure Cooked Salmon with Herbs 151

Instant Pot White Fish Curry 152

Pressure Roasted Tilapia 152

Instant Pot Roasted Salmon 153

Instant Pot Tilapia in Coconut Cream Sauce 153

Introduction

The Basics of Keto Diet

You've probably had a good number of keto diet pop-ups on your computer or have recently been seeing a lot of 'keto-friendly' signs in food stores and restaurants or you have a friend who's told they are embarking on this amazing diet called the ketogenic diet.

Well, while the keto diet has gained massive traction in the past 1-2 years or so, it has actually been in existence since the 1920s or earlier, but its documentation dates back to the 1920s. This diet was created as a treatment regimen for children who suffered from epilepsy. As it had a lot of success, it was adapted by many medical professionals to treat autism and bipolar among other neurological disorders.

Today, this fat-blasting diet is a firm favorite of people trying to lose weight and get in touch with their primal way of eating.

If we go back in history, carbs were not the primary food, and this explains why the first man and our ancestors led healthier lives and lived longer. It wasn't until the Agrarian Revolution that modern man tipped the healthy scales by introducing a lot of carbs that man could consume and everything that was being produced had to have some element of carbs.

The ketogenic diet helps us to go back to the basics and eat how we were supposed to eat from the very beginning. Keto is centered on fatty meals. All meals are primarily based on meats, seafood, poultry, cheeses, plant-based fat sources like avocado and nuts. Grains, both whole and refined, starchy veggies, most sugary fruits, dairy and legumes are eliminated from the diet.

In layman's terms, the keto diet is an even stricter version of the low-carb diet. When we take out the layers of the diet is where things get scientific and interesting. When done in the right way, the keto diet sends a signal of starvation to your brain which immediately launches the starvation metabolic state.

A lesson in biology

Okay, let me go back to the very beginning. Your body is primarily fueled by carbs that are in turn broken down into glucose in your digestive system. Glucose is what is stored by your muscle tissue and organs and is their main source of energy. When your body doesn't have any glucose to convert into energy, your body is forced to break down fat for energy using a process called ketosis (hence the name for the diet), where fat is broken down into ketone bodies that produce fuel for your body until your body gets carbohydrates, if it ever does.

The aim of the ketogenic diet is to train your body to shift focus from using carbohydrates for its primary source of energy to burning fat instead by use of ketone bodies that are produced by your liver.

An important point to note is that, significantly reducing your intake of carbs in a day doesn't mean that your body automatically shifts to ketosis. This can happen over a number of days as long as you stay consistent with the diet.

How low should you go?

Going into ketosis means you have to be super strict about the amount of carbs you take in. Well, how low you need to go ranges between 20 grams to 50 grams per day. Spoken in English, a ripe banana contains about 30 grams of carbs. A single slice of thin crust pizza contains about 30 grams of carbs as well. This means you have to be smart about the carbs you choose to add into your diet.

How does a keto meal look like?

So far, we have established that the keto diet is king in healthy fats, prince in protein and pauper in carbs. This means that your choice list includes cheeses, meats, nut butters, nuts, seeds, butter, and non-starchy veggies like broccoli, collard greens, asparagus, cauliflower, lettuce, kale, plant-based oils, and avocadoes. To sum it all up, you are supposed to eat about 4 grams of healthy fat for every gram of protein/carbohydrate which in essence means that about 80 percent of the calories you eat come from fats.

Why is the keto diet on everyone's lips?

Similar to the famous low-carb diet, Atkins, the sustainable weight loss benefits of the ketogenic diet outweigh those of low fat diets. Additionally, it does not allow gluten foods or sugar much like the Paleo diet. Healthy fats such as butter, avocado, coconut and omega-3s are emphasized and the famous bullet-proof coffee containing butter is also encouraged as a way to give you a burst of energy and limit hunger.

However, one major thing about the keto diet is it doesn't ease up on its carbohydrate restriction even after losing a good amount of weight. This is because, for you to remain in ketosis and to continue reaping these benefits, you have to keep your carb levels really low. While this may seem daunting to the average Joe who eats a ton of carbs at every meal, it's actually not as difficult as it seems.

Our bodies are very intelligent in the sense that, it is going to be difficult for your body to adjust to the high fat, low carb nature of the keto diet for the first 3-6 days but after that, you won't even crave carbs. You'll become so well adjusted that you will subconsciously gravitate towards low-carb food options without feeling like your body is missing something.

Keto diet and weight loss

It seems unlikely that a diet that is high in fat calories would actually help you lose weight as opposed to a diet that limits fat intake. However, with keto, your body burns fat rather than glucose from carbohydrate foods. Another fact to consider is the loss of water weight. Did you know that for every glucose molecule, there two water molecules attached to it?

This means that when you deplete the glucose stores in your body, you also lose a lot of water weight which you will notice within the first two weeks of your diet as actual loss of weight. **But, if it's water weight that you are losing, aren't you bound to gain it all back?**
NO!

For as long you stay on the keto diet, you are not going to gain back this weight because you will continue being on a low-carb diet. The best part of this high fat diet is that it keeps you full longer unlike a high–carb diet. Remember, your body is built to burn carbs fast in order to convert them to glucose which is then converted to energy. So, with the high-carb diet, you will inevitably be hungry by 11:00 am if you ate at 7:30 am. With the keto diet, you will soon find out that you don't need a mid-morning, afternoon or after-dinner snack.

Keto diet and health

Reducing your total carbohydrate intake to about 30 grams in a day, you automatically reduce your body's insulin surges, and you improve the glucose levels of your blood which inevitably reduces diabetic symptoms. So, if you have been struggling with diabetes, this is the diet for you.

Improved brain function is another major benefit of the keto diet. When your brain uses ketones for energy it helps it become more energy efficient as it doesn't have to work so hard for fuel. With sufficient fuel reserves, your brain will be more prepared to fight off disease-causing elements and also significantly reduce neurological stress.

Prepare your mind, body and soul

No pain, no gain, this is a common mantra for people who want to achieve something amazing in their lives. It recognizes that you have to go out of your way for you to achieve anything good in life. This is no different with the ketogenic diet. With all the amazing benefits we have seen from the diet, it is important to acknowledge that this is not going to be a walk in the park. It is not only very restrictive; it requires a lot of discipline for you to be able to do it correctly and in a safe way. We're not all cookies cut from the same dough, and so if you are planning to start the keto diet, it is important you see a nutritionist to guide on the safest low carb and protein measure per day. As we noted earlier some people can go as low as 20 grams while for others, the lowest they can go is 50 grams.

Do it the right way and you will be able to follow this diet for the rest of your life. Within the first two weeks of going into a keto diet, you are likely to experience the 'keto flu' which simply put is your body trying to resist this new way of life. Its common symptoms include constipation, light-headedness, bad breath with your tongue having a metallic taste, muscle cramps and severe loss of energy. It is therefore paramount that you work with a certified nutritionist to help you through the transition into ketosis and to also help tailor the keto diet to your nutritional needs.

Top 6 Keto Tips

Always read the labels: Today, food manufacturers seem to have found a way of sneaking carbs into almost everything. From condiments to meats and even veggies – the most unlikely of places. It's therefore important that you go through the labels of all the food you buy and go an extra mile to familiarize yourself with the carbohydrate count of foods that don't contain labels such as restaurant food. If for example you have a carb macro of up to 30 grams in a day, it is very easy to exceed this with hidden carbs. Did you know that a tablespoon of Heinz ketchup has about 4-5g of carbs?

Water, water and more water: As with any diet, water is very important to the keto diet. Don't wait until you are thirsty to drink water as this is already a sign that you are getting dehydrated. Make it a habit to carry along a water bottle and drink a glass of water every 1-2 hours. This not only helps with digestion; it also helps keep you full longer and adds a beautiful sheen to your skin and hair.

Don't fraternize with your food: What's the most common thing about keto adverts? Or better still, when you google keto lifestyle and open images, what do you see? I'll tell you, meaty and cheesy foods that make you feel that 'it's almost like Mc Donald's, I can do this!' typically, you see foods that are mostly forbidden in many other diets, minus the buns, in the case of a burger. But I will let you in on a tiny but important secret; you can eat bacon, cheese and a lot of meat on the keto diet, but guess what? Collard greens, broccoli and many other amazing veggies are also vital. Your aim should be to eat food that's as close as possible to their natural state. Avoid processed foods and eat exactly how Mother Nature intended for you to eat.

Expunge your pantry contents: Temptation is the primary enemy of any diet. Do yourself a favor and get rid of all carbs in your pantry and replace these with keto certified foods. Ready to eat snacks are the worst. Look for healthy keto snacks in our recipe section and get rid of all the junk.

Identify your restaurants beforehand: You are supposed to meet up with friends. Some suggest a pizza joint; others suggest pasta, and others taco. But you can't do any of these. Some classic keto friendly foods are salads, burgers minus the bun or a good old steak. Do a little homework on restaurants that have keto foods and when your buddies ask you where they can meet you for lunch or dinner, you don't feel stuck or come up with a fake excuse about why you can't meet them.

Set out a day where you do all your cooking: Following the keto diet on weekdays can be quite the challenge. You come home tired and starving and you have nothing to eat. It's very easy to get tempted to order Chinese from the restaurant down your block. The best solution is to do batch cooking on Sunday, for example, then divide it out for all the days of the week. This way, when you come home all you need to do is pop a batch in the microwave and a few Mins later, dinner is served. To help you with this, let us dive into our delicious and healthy keto recipes that will have you wondering why you never thought of this diet earlier!

Introduction to Instant Pot

Also referred to an electric pressure cooker, an instant pot is a cooking device that cooks food faster than other conventional cooking methods. It works by trapping steam by increasing the pressure inside the pot. The pressure increases the temperature which helps cook food faster. One of the notable benefits of an instant pot is that it saves energy.

Benefits of Using an Instant Pot

Cooking in an instant pot is a sure way of making tastier and healthier meals in a snap. All you need to do is throw all your ingredients in one pot to make the tastiest, well cooked meals in Mins. The following are some of the benefits of using an instant pot to cook:

- ✓ **Delicious and nutritious dishes:** Typically, fresh veggies and meats are cooked in the pot for a few Mins, at a high temperature. This technique releases and retains nutrition-packed juices from the meats and veggies as there is no escape through steam, meaning you not only get the best of nutrients but also flavors from the meals cooked in the instant pot.
- ✓ **Saves a lot of your time:** Perhaps the most attractive thing about using an electric pressure cooker is that you won't go crazy in the kitchen over a pot of food, checking it every few Mins to ensure it does not burn. The only thing you may be required to do with this cooker, especially if you are cooking meat, is to first brown it in some oil on manual high setting, if you want to have some great color in your stew; then, add in all the remaining ingredients in the pot and come back to it once the cooking time is over.
- ✓ **Timeless:** An instant pot is a kitchen device that you can use all year round and is not just limited to making hot bowls of stews and soup during winter. You can also use it to prepare tasty desserts and casseroles to be enjoyed during the summer, the beauty being that it can be used in place of an oven.
- ✓ **Easy to freeze:** Meals prepared in an instant pot can be packed and stored in the freezer for later use, saving you even more time.

Great Tips for Using Your Instant Pot

Thickening your sauce: The soups do not easily reduce when cooking with an instant pot, meaning that they also don't thicken. You may want to roll your meat chunks in flour (almond flour for keto dieters) before browning and add them to the pot if you like your sauce or soup nice and thick. Also, you can add a tablespoon or two of cornstarch-water mixture towards the end of cooking (preferably within the last five Mins of cooking time).

Go easy on the soup: As already mentioned, when cooking with an electric pressure cooker, the moisture does not evaporate since it cooks with a tightly locked lid throughout. When adapting a recipe that is usually cooked on a stove, it is advisable to reduce the cooking liquid by about a third, it should only cover the ingredients. Otherwise, overfilling your instant pot with soup may cause leakages from the top causing your food not to cook as well as it should.

Don't be a peeping Tom: Electric pressure cookers are designed to do their own thing. All you are required to do is throw in your ingredients, lock the lid, turn it on and let it to cook for the preselected period. If you are constantly checking the progress of your meal, you will have to increase the cooking time because every time you remove the lid, you reduce the pressure, ultimately reducing cooking temperature. It goes without saying, it is very dangerous to open an instant pot while the pressure is high, and your food will not be as tasty as it would had you trusted the cooker to do its thing!

INSTANT POT KETO POULTRY RECIPES

Healthy Marinara Chicken with Cauliflower Risotto

Yield: 4 | Total Time: 75 Mins | Prep Time: 10 Mins | Cook Time: 65 Mins

Ingredients

- 2 pounds boneless skinless chicken breast
- 3 tablespoons olive oil
- 4 small tomatoes, diced
- 4 cloves garlic
- 1 teaspoon oregano

- 1 teaspoon basil
- ½ teaspoon chili powder
- Dash garlic powder
- Dash pepper
- 1 cup chicken broth

Cauliflower Risotto

- 1/4 cup butter
- 8 ounces mushrooms, chopped
- 2 cloves garlic minced
- 12 ounces riced cauliflower
- 1/4 cup dry white wine

- 1/2 cup chicken broth
- 4 tablespoons heavy cream
- 1 cup grated parmesan cheese
- Salt & pepper

Directions:

1. **Prepare Risotto:** Melt butter in a large pan; sauté garlic and mushrooms until tender and lightly brown. Season with salt and pepper and lower heat to medium low. Stir in cauliflower and then add white wine. Cook for a few Mins or until liquid is evaporated. Stir in broth and cook for about 3 Mins. Stir in cream and cook, covered, until cauliflower is tender. Stir in parmesan until melted and remove from heat. Serve sprinkled with more parmesan.
2. Set your instant pot to manual high and heat the oil. Sprinkle chicken with garlic powder, salt and pepper; fry in the pot for 2 Mins per side or until browned. Add in the remaining ingredients and lock lid. Cook on high for 20 Mins and then let pressure come down on its own.
3. Serve warm.

Nutrition : Calories: 197; Total Fat: 16.9 g; Carbs: 7.5 g; Dietary Fiber: 2.4 g; Sugars: 2.7 g; Protein: 26.2 g; Cholesterol: 76 mg; Sodium: 92 mg

Buffalo Chicken Fingers with Nutty Kale Salad

Yield: 4 | Total Time: 35 Mins | Prep Time: 10 Mins | Cook Time: 25 Mins

Ingredients

- 2 pounds chicken, sliced into strips
- 4 tablespoons fresh lemon juice
- 2 tablespoons hot sauce

Salad

- 2 tablespoons extra virgin olive oil
- 1 pound Lacinato kale, sliced into thin strips

- Breadcrumbs
- Pinch of salt & black pepper
- ½ cup chicken broth

- 1/2 cup roasted almonds
- Pinch of sea salt
- Pinch of pepper

Directions:

1. Prepare salad: Place kale in a bowl and add olive oil; massage olive oil with hands into kale until kale is tender; sprinkle with salt and pepper and toss with toasted almonds.
2. Marinate chicken in fresh lemon juice and salt for a few hours and then coat with crushed crumbs; fry in an instant pot set on sauté mode for about 5 Mins or until browned. Stir in broth and lock lid. Cook on high for 20 Mins and let pressure come down naturally. Toss with black pepper and hot sauce and serve with raw celery, garnish with parsley.

Nutrition : Calories: 169; Total Fat: 3.6 g; Carbs: 1.8 g; Dietary Fiber: 0.4 g; Sugars: 1.6 g; Protein: 29.6g; Cholesterol: 77 mg; Sodium: 869 mg

Healthy Roasted Turkey with Low Carb Avocado Relish

Yield: 6 | Total Time: 1 Hour 40 Mins | Prep Time: 10 Mins | Cook Time: 1 Hour 30 Mins

Ingredients:

- 3 tablespoons extra-virgin olive oil
- ½ cup apple cider vinegar
- 3 cloves garlic, minced
- 2-3 tablespoons minced ginger
- 2 pounds whole turkey

Avocado Relish

- ½ avocado, diced, 1 seedless grapefruit cut into segments discarding the membranes
- 1 small Vidalia onion, minced

- 1-pound chopped carrots
- handful of rosemary
- Pinch of sea salt
- Pinch of pepper

- 1 tsp. red wine vinegar
- 1 tbsp. fresh cilantro, chopped
- 1 tsp natural honey

Directions:

1. Place turkey in aluminum foil. In a bowl, whisk together olive oil, apple cider vinegar, garlic, and ginger until well combined; pour over the turkey and top with carrots and rosemary. Sprinkle with salt and pepper and fold to wrap well. Add water to an instant pot and insert a metal trivet. Place the foil over the trivet and cook on high for 1 ½ hours. Let pressure come down naturally.
2. **Prepare Relish:** Combine the avocado, grapefruit segments, onion, honey, vinegar and cilantro and toss well to combine.
3. Serve turkey with the avocado relish.

Nutrition : Calories: 331; Total Fat: 18.7 g; Carbs: 6.3 g; Dietary Fiber: 1.8 g; Sugars: 2.5 g; Protein: 37.4 g; Cholesterol: 122 mg; Sodium: 225 mg

Instant Pot Healthy Turkey Meat Balls

Yield: 4 | Total Time: 20 Mins | Prep Time: 10 Mins | Cook Time: 10 Mins

Ingredients

- 2 tablespoons olive oil
- 1-pound ground turkey
- 1/2 cup crushed cheese crackers
- 1 teaspoon minced onion
- 1 tablespoon red pepper flakes
- 1 tablespoon garlic powder
- 1 egg

Directions

1. In a bowl, mix together all ingredients until well combined; form four large patties from the mixture. Set your instant pot on manual high and add in oil; cook the patties for 5 Mins per side or until cooked through. Lock lid and cook the patties for 5 Mins. Let pressure come down naturally.

Nutrition : Calories: 239; Total Fat: 17.2g; Carbs: 7.6g; Dietary Fiber: Sugars: Protein: 25.5g; Cholesterol: 131mg; Sodium: 160m

Delicious Turkey Sausage Patties with Lemon Tahini Sauce

Yield: 8 | Total Time: 26 Mins | Prep Time: 10 Mins | Cook Time: 16 Mins

Ingredients

- 2 pounds ground turkey
- 1/4 teaspoon cayenne pepper
- 3/4 teaspoon ground ginger
- 1 teaspoon dried sage
- 1 1/2 teaspoons salt
- 1 1/2 teaspoons pepper
- 4 cups of green salad for serving

Low Carb Lemon Tahini Sauce

- 4 tablespoons lemon juice
- ½ cup organic tahini
- 1 tablespoon olive oil
- 2 cloves garlic
- ⅓ cup water
- A pinch sea & pepper

Directions

1. Prepare Tahini: in a blender, blend together all ingredients until very smooth. Refrigerate until ready to use.
2. Mix together ground turkey, cayenne pepper, sage, ginger, salt and pepper in a bowl until well blended. Form patties from the mixture and place on a plate.
3. Set your instant pot on manual high and add in oil; cook the patties for 5 Mins per side or until cooked through. Lock lid and cook the patties for 5 Mins. Let pressure come down naturally. Serve the turkey patties with green salad drizzled with lemon tahini.

Nutrition : Calories: 169; Total Fat: 18.6g; Carbs: 1.5g; Dietary Fiber: Sugars: Protein: 22.5g; Cholesterol: 84mg; Sodium: 500mg

Instant Pot Roast Chicken with Steamed Veggies

Yield: 4 | Total Time: 1 Hour 40 Mins | Prep Time: 10 Mins | Cook Time: 1 Hour 30 Mins

Ingredients

- 1.5 kg chicken
- 3 heads garlic, cut in half across
- 3 brown onions, cut into wedges
- 200g cauliflower
- 2 tbsp. chicken seasoning blend: Mix together ½ tsp. each of crushed dried rosemary, paprika, dry mustard powder, garlic powder, ground dried thyme, ground black pepper, 1 tsp. dried basil, 1 ½ tsp. sea salt, ¼ tsp. celery seeds, ¼ tsp. dried parsley, 1/8 tsp. each of cayenne pepper, ground cumin, and chicken bouillon granules.
- 200g broccoli
- 200g green beans
- 1 pouch cheese sauce

Directions

1. Add water to an instant pot and insert a metal trivet.
2. On aluminum foil, combine garlic and onion; sprinkle with olive oil.
3. Rub the chicken seasoning blend into the chicken and place it on top of the bed of garlic and onion; fold the foil to wrap the contents and place over the trivet. Lock lid and cook on high for 90 Mins. Release pressure naturally.
4. Place the beans into a steamer and add cauliflower and broccoli; steam for about 10 Mins or until tender.
5. Serve the chicken and steamed veggies on a plate; heat the cheese sauce and pour over the veggies. Enjoy!

Nutrition : Calories: 665; Fat: 46.6g; Carbs: 11.2g; Protein: 49.1g

Healthy Chicken Curry

Yield: 1 Serving | Total Time: 30 Mins | Prep Time: 10 Mins | Cook Time: 20 Mins

Ingredients

- 1 tablespoon olive oil
- 100 grams chicken, diced
- ¼ cup chicken broth
- Pinch of turmeric
- Dash of onion powder
- 1 tablespoon minced red onion
- Pinch of garlic powder
- ¼ teaspoon curry powder
- Pinch of sea salt
- Pinch of pepper
- Stevia
- Pinch of cayenne
- 1 cup riced cauliflower
- 1 tablespoon butter
- 1 red onion

Directions

1. Prepare cauliflower by melting butter in a skillet and then sautéing red onion. Stir in cauliflower and cook for about 4 Mins or until tender. Set aside until ready to serve.
2. Set an instant pot on sauté mode, heat oil and sauté onion and garlic; stir in chicken and cook until browned. Stir spices in chicken broth and Stevia and add to the pot. Lock lid and cook on high for 15 Mins. Release the pressure naturally and serve hot over sautéed cauliflower.

Nutrition : Calories: 213; Fat: 17.4g; Carbs: 2.3g; Protein: 20.5g

Low Carb Turkey Served with Creamy Sauce and Sautéed Capers

Yield: 4 | Total Time: 40 Mins | Prep Time: 15 Mins | Cook Time: 25 Mins

Ingredients

- 2 pounds turkey breast
- 1/3 cup small capers
- 1 cup cream cheese
- 2 cups sour cream
- 2 tbsp. butter
- 1 tbsp. tamari sauce
- A pinch of sea salt
- A pinch of pepper

Directions

1. Set your instant pot on manual high; heat half of the butter; season turkey with salt and pepper and fry until golden brown. Add in cream cheese and sour cream; bring to a gentle boil and then simmer until the sauce is thick. Season the sauce with tamari, salt and pepper; lock lid and cook on high for 5 Mins. Let pressure come down naturally.
2. Melt the remaining butter in a pan and sauté the capers over high heat until crispy.
3. Serve the turkey meat with the fried capers and creamy sauce. Enjoy!

Nutrition : Calories: 498; Fat: 34.1g; Carbs: 7.9g; Protein: 39g

Tasty Instant Pot Thai Turkey Legs

Yield: 4 | Total Time: 1 Hour 12 Mins | Prep Time: 7 Mins | Cook Time: 1 Hour 5 Mins

Ingredients

- 1-pound turkey legs
- 2 cups coconut milk
- 1 tbsp. lime juice
- 1½ tsp. lemon garlic seasoning
- Lime wedges
- ¼ cup fresh cilantro
- 1 tsp. ghee

Directions

1. Set your instant pot to manual high and melt in ghee; sauté turkey until browned and then stir in coconut milk, lime juice, lime wedge, lemon garlic seasoning, and cilantro. Add the turkey legs and lock lid. Cook on high for 1 hour and then let pressure come down on its own.

Nutritional Information per Serving:

Calories: 524; Total Fat: 40.8 g; Carbs: 7.6 g; Dietary Fiber: 2.7 g; Sugars: 4.2 g; Protein: 34.4 g; Cholesterol: 99 mg; Sodium: 106 mg

Gingery Roasted Turkey

Yield: 6 | Total Time: 1 Hour 10 Mins | Prep Time: 10 Mins | Cook Time: 1 Hour

Ingredients:

- 3 tablespoons extra-virgin olive oil
- ½ cup apple cider vinegar
- 3 cloves garlic, minced
- 2-3 tablespoons minced ginger
- 2 pounds whole turkey
- 1 pound chopped carrots
- handful of rosemary
- Pinch of sea salt
- Pinch of pepper

Directions:

1. Set your instant pot to high sauté setting and add in turkey; In a bowl, whisk together olive oil, apple cider vinegar, garlic, and ginger until well combined; pour over the turkey and top with carrots and rosemary. Sprinkle with salt and pepper and lock lid; select manual and set pressure to high for 1 hour. When ready, release the pressure naturally. Serve warm.

Nutrition : Calories: 372; Total Fat: 24.6 g; Carbs: 7.6 g; Dietary Fiber: 1.7 g; Sugars: 3.3 g; Protein: 50 g; Cholesterol: 151 mg; Sodium: 220 mg

Herbed Instant Pot Turkey Breast

Yield: 2 | Total Time: 1Hour 10 Mins | Prep Time: 10 Mins | Cook Time: 1 Hour

Ingredients

- 1-pound turkey breast
- ¼ cup whipped cream cheese, spread with garden veggies
- 2 tbsp. softened butter
- 1 tbsp. soy sauce
- ½ tsp. dried basil
- 1 tbsp. minced parsley
- ½ tsp. dried thyme
- ½ tsp. dried sage
- ¼ tsp. garlic powder
- ¼ tsp sea salt
- ¼ tsp. ground black pepper

Directions

1. In a small bowl, combine all the ingredients, except turkey, until well blended; brush the mixture over the turkey breast and place in your instant pot. Lock lid and cook on high setting for 1 hour. Naturally release the pressure and then serve.

Nutrition : Calories: 374; Total Fat: 15.7 g; Carbs: 12.7 g; Dietary Fiber: 1.5 g; Sugars: 8.3 g; Protein: 43.7 g; Cholesterol: 130 mg; Sodium: 3228 mg

Tangy Instant Pot Turkey Meatballs

Yield: 6 | Total Time: 1 Hours 30 Mins | Prep Time: 30 Mins | Cook Time: 1 Hour

Ingredients

For meatballs
- 1-pound ground turkey
- ½ cup panko breadcrumbs
- ½ tsp. onion powder
- ½ tsp. chili powder
- ½ tsp. garlic salt
- 1 egg

For sauce
- 2 ½ tbsp. raw honey
- 1 cup tomato sauce
- 2 tbsp. white vinegar
- 2 tbsp. Worcestershire sauce
- ½ tsp. onion powder
- ½ tsp. chili powder
- ½ tsp. garlic salt

Directions

1. In a bowl, mix ground turkey, breadcrumbs, onion powder, garlic salt, chili powder, and egg until well combined; roll the mixture into 1-inch balls and arrange them on a greased heatproof dish that fits in your pot. Add water to your instant pot and put in a metal trivet; place the dish with the meatballs over the trivet and lock lid. Cook on high setting for 1 hour and then naturally release the pressure.

Nutrition : Calories: 307; Total Fat: 13.8 g; Carbs: 13.4 g; Dietary Fiber: 1.3 g; Sugars: 8.3 g; Protein: 33.7 g; Cholesterol: 157 mg; Sodium: 548 mg

Pressure Roasted Chicken

Yield: 6 | Total Time: 1 Hour 40 Mins | Prep Time: 10 Mins | Cook Time: 1 Hour 30 Mins

Ingredients:
- 1 tablespoon extra-virgin olive oil
- ½ cup apple cider vinegar
- 3 cloves garlic, minced
- 2-3 tablespoons minced ginger
- 2 pounds whole chicken
- 1 pound chopped carrots
- handful of rosemary
- Pinch of sea salt
- Pinch of pepper

Directions

1. Place chicken in your instant pot. In a bowl, whisk together olive oil, apple cider vinegar, garlic, and ginger until well combined; pour over the chicken and top with carrots and rosemary. Sprinkle with salt and pepper and lock lid. Cook on high setting for 1 ½ hours and then let pressure come down on its own. Serve warm over steamed veggies.

Nutrition : Calories: 372; Total Fat: 14.6 g; Carbs: 7.6 g; Dietary Fiber: 1.7 g; Sugars: 3.3 g; Protein: 50 g; Cholesterol: 151 mg; Sodium: 220 mg

Tasty Instant Pot Turkey Breast

Yield: 2 | Total Time: 1 Hour 10 Mins | Prep Time: 10 Mins | Cook Time: 1 Hour

Ingredients

- 1-pound turkey breast (bone-in)
- 1-ounce dry onion soup mix

Directions

1. Rinse turkey and pat it dry; rub the soup mix under and outside the skin and place it in your instant pot. Lock lid and cook on high setting for 1 hour. Let pressure come down on its own.

Nutrition : Calories: 227; Total Fat: 3.8 g; Carbs: 8.8g; Dietary Fiber: 2.1 g; Sugars: 6.6 g; Protein: 39.8 g; Cholesterol: 98 mg; Sodium: 3440 mg

Pressure Cooked Cajun Chicken with Lime Butter Steamed Veggies

Yield: 2 | Total Time: 30 Mins | Prep Time: 10 Mins | Cook Time: 20 Mins

Ingredients

- 12 ounces boneless skinless chicken breast
- 2 teaspoons water
- 1 tablespoon cayenne pepper

- ½ teaspoon sea salt
- ¼ teaspoon pepper
- ½ teaspoon onion powder
- ½ teaspoon garlic powder

Lime Butter Steamed Veggies

- 3 cups cut-up fresh assorted vegetables (cauliflower, broccoli florets, and sliced carrots)
- 1 tbsp. fresh lime juice
- 1 tsp. chopped jalapeño pepper

- 1 small clove garlic, chopped
- 2 tbsp. butter
- 1 tsp. grated lime peel
- ½ tsp. salt

Directions:

1. **Prepare Veggies:** In a saucepan, melt butter over medium low heat; add garlic and sauté for about 1 minute or until fragrant. Stir in lime juice, lime peel, jalapeño pepper, and salt; mix well and set aside. Place steamer in a large saucepan and add a cup of water; bring to a boil. Add the veggies to the steamer and cook, covered, for about 5 Mins or until crisp and tender. Place the steamed veggies in a serving bowl and pour over the butter sauce; toss to coat well and serve.
2. Stir all spices into water and rub onto chicken; let marinate for at least 1hour. Heat a tablespoon of oil in the instant pot and fry the chicken until browned. Remove the chicken and add in broth. Insert a metal trivet into the pot and place the chicken over the trivet. Lock lid and cook on manual high for 10 Mins. Let pressure come down on its own. Serve grilled chicken over steamed veggies. Enjoy!

Nutrition : Calories: 337; Total Fat: 13.1 g; Carbs: 2.7 g; Dietary Fiber: 0.9 g; Sugars: 0.7 g; Protein: 49.7 g; Cholesterol: 151 mg; Sodium: 616 mg

Instant Pot Ginger Peach Chicken

Yield: 2 | Total Time: 1 Hour 10 Mins | Prep Time: 10 Mins | Cook Time: 1 Hour

Ingredients

- 1-pound chicken thighs, boneless, skinless
- 2 cloves garlic, minced
- 2 tablespoons olive oil
- 1-inch fresh ginger root, grated
- 1 tbsp. low-sodium soy sauce
- 2 tablespoons peach jam

Directions

1. Place the chicken thighs in your instant pot.
2. In a small bowl, mix ginger, garlic, olive oil, peach jam, and soy sauce until well blended; spoon the sauce over the chicken and cover the pot with lid; cook on high setting for 1 hour and then let pressure come down on its own. Remove the chicken from the pot and shred. Return and let sit for a few Mins to mix with juice. Serve with steamed veggies.

Nutrition : Calories: 386; Total Fat: 13.8 g; Carbs: 13.8g; Dietary Fiber: 3.1 g; Sugars: 7.6 g; Protein: 33.4 g; Cholesterol: 101 mg; Sodium: 337 mg

Instant Pot Asian chicken lettuce wraps

Yields: 2 | Total Time: 1 Hour 5 Mins | Prep Time: 5 Mins | Cook Time: 1 Hour

Ingredients

- 1-pound ground chicken
- 2 minced cloves garlic
- 2 large carrots, grated
- 1 medium red bell pepper, diced
- 1 teaspoon Stevia
- 1/4 cup low-sodium soy sauce
- 1/4 tsp. crushed red pepper flakes
- 1/4 cup ketchup

Directions

1. Combine all ingredients in your instant pot and cook on high setting for 1 hour. Shred the chicken and return to the pot. Stir to mix well and divide among lettuce leaves. Roll to form wraps and serve.

Nutrition : Calories: 262; Total Fat: 8.6 g; Carbs: 11.1g; Dietary Fiber: 1.4 g; Sugars: 7.7 g; Protein: 34.8 g; Cholesterol: 101 mg; Sodium: 1170 mg

Oregano Chicken with Sautéed Kale

Yield: 4 | Total Time: 30 Mins | Prep Time: 10 Mins | Cook Time: 20 Mins

Ingredients

- 2 pounds chicken breast
- 3 tablespoons olive oil
- 1 cup chicken broth
- 1 teaspoon dried oregano
- ¼ teaspoon onion powder
- ¼ teaspoon garlic powder
- Pinch of salt & pepper
- ½ cup breadcrumbs
- 4 cups kale, chopped
- 2 tablespoons butter
- 2 red onions, chopped

Directions:

1. Mix dry spices with crumbs; dip chicken in olive oil and dust with bread crumb mix.
2. Add broth to the instant pot and then insert a metal trivet. Place the chicken over the trivet and lock lid; cook on manual high for 20 Mins.
3. Add butter to a skillet over medium heat and sauté red onion until fragrant; stir in kale and cook for about 3 Mins or until just wilted; season with salt and pepper. Serve the chicken over the fried kale.

Nutrition : Calories: 133; Total Fat: 13 g; Carbs: 2.3 g; Dietary Fiber: 0.8 g; Sugars: 0.6 g; Protein: 22.8 g; Cholesterol: 64 mg; Sodium: 243 mg

Tasty Citric Chicken with Fried Button Mushrooms

Yield: 4 | Total Time: 1 Hour 10 Mins | Prep Time: 10 Mins | Cook Time: 1 Hour

Ingredients

- 2 pounds chicken breast
- 1 red onion, minced
- Juice of ½ lemon
- Pinch of lemon zest
- Pinch of saffron
- Pinch of ground coriander
- Pinch of ginger
- Pinch of salt & pepper
- Lemon slices
- 2 cups button mushrooms
- 2 tablespoons butter
- 2 red onions, chopped

Directions:

1. Soak saffron in fresh lemon juice; crush into paste and then add dry spices.
2. Dip in chicken and rub remaining spices into chicken; sprinkle with salt and pepper and wrap in foil. Add water to an instant pot and insert a trivet; place the chicken over the trivet, lock lid and cook on manual high for 1 hour.
3. Add butter to a skillet over medium heat and sauté red onion until fragrant; stir in mushrooms and cook for about 6 Mins or until tender. Season with salt and pepper. Serve the chicken over the mushrooms.

Nutrition : Calories: 122; Total Fat: 2.6 g; Carbs: 1.9 g; Dietary Fiber: 0.5 g; Sugars: 0.6 g; Protein: 21.4 g; Cholesterol: 64 mg; Sodium: 52 mg

Low Carb Turkey Ratatouille

Yield: 4 | Total Time: 40 Mins | Prep Time: 15 Mins | Cook Time: 25 Mins

Ingredients

- 4 tablespoons extra-virgin olive oil
- 2 pounds boneless turkey cutlet
- 1 cup mushrooms
- 1 sweet red pepper
- 1 medium zucchini
- 1 eggplant
- 1/2 cup tomato puree
- 1 tsp garlic
- 1 tsp leaf basil
- 1/8 tsp salt
- 1/2 teaspoon sweetener
- 1/8 tsp black pepper

Directions

1. Set your instant pot to manual high and heat oil; sprinkle the meat with salt and pepper and sauté for about 3 Mins per side; transfer to a plate and add the remaining oil to the pot. Sauté red pepper, zucchini and eggplant for about 5 Mins. Stir in garlic, mushrooms, basil, tomato puree. Cook for 5 Mins and then stir in turkey, salt and pepper. Lock lid and cook on high for 15 Mins. Let pressure come down on its own. Serve hot.

Nutrition : Calories: 568; Total Fat: 25.8 g; Carbs: 13.4g; Dietary Fiber: 5.8 g; Sugars: 7.6 g; Protein: 69.6 g; Cholesterol: 172 mg; Sodium: 250 mg

Spiced Chicken Patties Low Carb Lemon Pesto

Yield: 4 | Total Time: 40 Mins | Prep Time: 10 Mins | Cook Time: 30 Mins

Ingredients

- 4 tablespoons olive oil
- 400 grams ground chicken breast
- 1 clove garlic, minced
- ½ red onion, minced
- Dash of garlic powder
- Dash of onion powder
- Pinch of cayenne pepper
- Pinch of salt & pepper

Low Carb Lemon Pesto

- 1 tablespoon fresh lemon juice
- 2 tablespoons lemon zest, chopped
- 1/2 cup grated parmesan cheese
- 5 cloves garlic, chopped
- 1/4 cup pine nuts
- 1/2 cup extra virgin olive oil
- 2 cups basil leaves, packed
- Pinch of salt & pepper

Directions:

1. Prepare pesto: blend together all ingredients in a blender until very smooth; refrigerate until ready to use.
2. In a small bowl, mix all ingredients until well combined; form patties and set aside. Set your instant pot to manual high and heat in oil; fry in a saucepan, deglazing with water to keep chicken moist. Lock lid and cook the patties for 5 Mins on high setting. Let pressure come down on its own. Serve with lemon pesto.

Nutrition : Calories: 414; Total Fat: 20.9 g; Carbs: 11.6 g; Dietary Fiber: 0.4 g; Sugars: 0.6 g; Protein: 25.2 g; Cholesterol: 63 mg; Sodium: 50 mg

Vegetable & Chicken Stir-Fry

Yield: 4 | Total Time: 20 Mins | Prep Time: 10 Mins | Cook Time: 10 Mins

Ingredients

- 4 chicken breasts (butterfly), marinate in egg white overnight
- 2 cups red pepper
- 2 cups mange tout
- 2 cups grated carrot
- 2 cups broccoli
- 2 cups almonds
- 2 cloves of garlic
- ½ tsp. ginger
- 2 tbsp. soya sauce
- 125ml chicken stock.
- 2 tbsp. coconut oil

Directions

1. Heat coconut oil in your instant pot. Sauté the garlic and ginger until fragrant.
2. Cook the chicken breast in the oil until browned and then add the vegetables. Toss and cook until almost done.
3. Add 2 tbsp. soya sauce and chicken stock. Lock lid and cook on manual high for 5 Mins. Let pressure come down on its own.

Nutrition : Calories: 186; Total Fat: 11 g; Carbs: 4 g; Dietary Fiber: 1.5 g; Sugars: 1.9 g; Protein: 17 g; Cholesterol: 550 mg; Sodium: 1272 mg

Turkey-Cauliflower Hash with Avocado and Hardboiled Egg

Yield: 4 | Total Time: 40 Mins | Prep Time: 20 Mins | Cook Time: 20 Mins

Ingredients

- 2 tablespoons butter stick
- 2 pounds turkey meat
- 1 small onion
- 3 cups cauliflower
- 1 tsp thyme
- 1/4 cup heavy cream
- 1/2 tsp salt
- 1/8 tsp pepper
- 4 hardboiled eggs, chopped
- 1 avocado, diced

Directions

1. Bring a pot of salted water to a rolling boil; add cauliflower and cook for 4 Mins or until tender; drain and let cool before chopping coarsely.
2. In the meantime, melt butter in an instant pot and sauté onion and thyme; season with salt and pepper; add cauliflower and cook for 2 Mins. Stir in turkey meat; cook for about 6 Mins or until browned. Stir in cream and lock lid. Cook for 10 Mins and let pressure come down on its own. Serve topped with chopped boiled eggs and avocado.

Nutrition : Calories: 397; Fat: 32.2g; Carbs: 16.2g; Protein: 28.9g

Instant Pot Chicken Curry

Yield: 1 Serving | Total Time: 35 Mins | Prep Time: 10 Mins | Cook Time: 25 Mins

Ingredients

- 4 tbsp. coconut oil
- 100 grams chicken, diced
- ¼ cup chicken broth
- Pinch of turmeric
- Dash of onion powder
- 1 tablespoon minced red onion
- Pinch of garlic powder
- ¼ teaspoon curry powder
- Pinch of sea salt
- Pinch of pepper
- Stevia
- Pinch of cayenne

Directions

1. Set your instant pot to manual high, melt coconut oil and then stir in garlic and onion. Cook until fragrant and stir in chicken. In a small bowl, stir together spices, Stevia, and chicken broth until dissolved, stir into the chicken and lock lid. Cook for 20 Mins and then naturally release the pressure. Serve hot.

Nutrition : Calories: 170; Total Fat: 23.5 g; Carbs: 5.3 g; Dietary Fiber: 0.6 g; Sugars: 0.8 g; Protein: 30.5 g; Cholesterol: 77 mg; Sodium: 255 mg

Healthy Turkey Loaf with Sautéed Button Mushrooms

Yield: 2 | Total Time: 45 Mins | Prep Time: 15 Mins | Cook Time: 30 Mins

Ingredients

- 2 eggs
- 1-pound ground turkey
- 1/2 cup chopped onion
- 1/4 cup chopped yellow bell pepper
- 1/4 cup chopped red bell pepper
- 1/2 cup salsa
- 1/4 cup dry breadcrumbs
- A pinch of lemon pepper
- 1 cup button mushrooms
- 1 tablespoon olive oil
- 1 red onion

Directions

1. In a bowl, mix together bell peppers, breadcrumbs, salsa, egg, turkey, onion and lemon pepper until well blended. Roll the mixture to form a loaf. Add water to an instant pot and insert a metal trivet; place the meatloaf over the trivet and lock lid. Cook on high setting for 25 Mins and then transfer the meatloaf to oven. Bake at 450 degrees for 5 Mins or until golden browned.
2. Meanwhile, heat olive oil in a skillet; sauté red onion until fragrant; stir in button mushrooms and cook until tender. Serve the meatloaf topped with sautéed mushrooms for a healthy satisfying meal.

Nutrition : Calories: 112; fat: 5.1 g; carbohydrates: 6.1 g; protein: 10.3 g; cholesterol; 73 mg; sodium: 174 mg

Satisfying Turkey Lettuce Wraps

Yields: 4 | Total Time: 50 Mins | Prep Time: 15 Mins | Cook Time: 35 Mins

Ingredients

- 1/2 lb. ground turkey
- 1/2 small onion, finely chopped
- 1 garlic clove, minced
- 2 tablespoons extra virgin olive oil
- 1 head lettuce
- 1 teaspoon cumin
- 1/2 tablespoon fresh ginger, sliced
- 2 tablespoons apple cider vinegar
- 2 tablespoons freshly chopped cilantro
- 1 teaspoon freshly ground black pepper
- 1 teaspoon sea salt

Directions

1. Add oil to your instant pot and set it on sauté mode; add in garlic and onion and cook until fragrant and translucent. Add turkey and lock lid; cook for about 5 Mins. Stir in the remaining ingredients and lock lid; cook on high for 30 Mins and then quick release the pressure.
2. To serve, ladle a spoonful of turkey mixture onto a lettuce leaf and wrap. Enjoy!

Nutrition : Calories: 192; Total Fat: 13.6 g; Carbs: 4.6 g; Dietary Fiber: 1 g; Sugars: 1.2 g Protein: 16.3 g; Cholesterol: 58 mg; Sodium: 535 mg

Lemon Olive Chicken

Yield: 4 | Total Time: 30 Mins | Prep Time: 10 Mins | Cook Time: 20 Mins

Ingredients

- 4 boneless skinless chicken breasts
- ½ cup coconut oil
- ¼ tsp. black pepper
- ½ tsp. cumin
- 1tsp. sea salt
- 1cup chicken bone broth
- 2 tbsp. fresh lemon juice
- ½ cup red onion, sliced
- 1can pitted green olives
- 1/2 lemon, thinly sliced

Directions

1. Generously season chicken breasts with cumin, pepper and salt; set your instant pot on sauté mode and heat the coconut oil; add chicken and brown both sides. Stir in the remaining ingredients; bring to a gentle simmer and then lock lid.
2. Cook on high for 10 Mins and then use quick release method to release pressure.

Nutrition : Calories: 420; Total Fat: 38.7 g; Carbs: 0.6 g; Dietary Fiber: 0.2 g; Sugars: 0.2 g; Protein: 42.4 g; Cholesterol: 130 mg; Sodium: 662 mg

Instant Pot Turkey with Veggies

Yield: 4 | Total Time: 20 Mins | Prep Time: 15 Mins | Cook Time: 5 Mins

Ingredients

- 1 tablespoon extra-virgin olive oil
- 6 ounces turkey
- ¼ cup capers
- ¼ cup diced fresh tomatoes
- Steamed green beans for serving

Directions

1. Heat oil in your instant pot; add turkey and lock lid. Cook on high for 5 Mins and then let pressure come down.
2. Remove the cooked turkey from the pot and transfer to a plate; add capers and tomatoes to the pan and cook until juicy. Spoon the caper mixture over the turkey and serve with steamed green beans.

Nutrition : Calories: 111; Total Fat: 5.7g; Carbs: 1.8g; Dietary Fiber: 0.9g; Protein: 5.7g; Cholesterol: 32mg; Sodium: 286mg; sugars: 0.5g

Instant Pot Baked Chicken with Salsa

Yield: 1 Serving | Total Time: 55 Mins | Prep Time: 20 Mins | Cook Time: 35 Mins

Ingredients:

- Juice of 1/4 lemon
- 2 teaspoons ground turmeric
- 1 tablespoon extra-virgin olive oil
- 4 ounces chicken breast, skinless, boneless
- ¼ cup chopped kale
- 1 teaspoon chopped ginger
- 1 large red onion, sliced
- ¼ cup buckwheat

For the salsa

- 1 large tomato, finely chopped
- 1 tablespoon capers, finely chopped
- 1 bird's eye chili, finely chopped
- Juice of 1/4 lemon
- ½ cup parsley, finely chopped

Directions

1. Make salsa: mix chopped tomato, capers, chili, lemon juice, and parsley in a large bowl.
2. In a large bowl, mix lemon juice, 1 teaspoon turmeric, and a splash of extra virgin olive oil; add the chicken and stir to combine well. Marinate for about 10 Mins.
3. Set your instant pot to high sauté setting and add in oil; place the chicken in the pot and cook for about 4 Mins per side or until evenly browned. Remove the chicken and place a metal trivet in your pot and add in chicken broth; place the chicken over the trivet and lock lid; select manual and set pressure to high for 25 Mins. When ready, release the pressure naturally and then remove chicken from the pot; keep warm.
4. In the meantime, steam kale in a steamer for about 5 Mins.
5. Fry ginger and red onion in a splash of extra virgin olive oil until tender; stir in kale and cook for about 1 minute.
6. Follow package instructions to cook buckwheat with the remaining turmeric.
7. Serve the buckwheat with chicken, veggies and salsa.

Nutrition : Calories: 335; Total Fat: 11.6g; Carbs: 2.6g; Dietary Fiber: 4.3g; Protein: 22.5g; Cholesterol: 51mg; Sodium: 224mg; sugars: 5.8g

Instant Pot Crunchy Chicken Salad

Yield: 2 | Total Time: 45 Mins | Prep Time: 10 Mins | Cook Time: 35 Mins

Ingredients

- 250g chicken
- ¼ cup Tamari soy sauce
- 1 tablespoon avocado oil
- 1 tablespoon Olive oil
- ½ tablespoon lemon juice, freshly squeezed
- 4 Radishes, sliced
- 6 cherry tomatoes, halved
- ½ red bell pepper, sliced
- 2 cups salad greens
- ½ teaspoon salt

Directions

1. Pour tamari sauce in a large bowl; add in steak and toss to coat well; cover and let marinate for a few hours before cooking.
2. In another bowl, combine green salad, radishes, tomatoes, bell peppers, lemon juice, olive oil and salt; toss to coat well and set aside.
3. Set your instant pot to high sauté setting and add in oil; place the chicken in the pot and cook for about 4 Mins per side or until evenly browned. Remove the chicken and place a metal trivet in your pot and add in chicken broth; place the chicken over the trivet and lock lid; select manual and set pressure to high for 25 Mins. When ready, release the pressure naturally and then remove chicken from the pot; let cool for a minute before slicing to serve. Divide the salad between two plates and top each with chicken slices.

Nutrition : Calories: 356; Total Fat: 37.1g; Carbs: 6g; Dietary Fiber: 4.3g; sugars: 1.8g Protein: 33.5g; Cholesterol: 51mg; Sodium: 224mg

Pressure Cooked Chicken Shawarma

Yield: 6 | Total Time: 25 Mins | Prep Time: 10 Mins | Cook Time: 15 Mins

Ingredients

- 1-pound chicken thighs
- 1-pound chicken breasts, sliced
- 1/8 tsp. cinnamon
- 1/4 tsp. chili powder
- 1 tsp. ground cumin
- 1/4 tsp. ground allspice
- 1/4 tsp. granulated garlic
- 1/2 tsp. turmeric
- 1 tsp. paprika
- Pinch of salt
- Pinch of pepper
- 1 cup chicken broth

Directions

1. Mix all ingredients in your instant pot and lock lid; cook on poultry setting for 15 Mins and then release pressure naturally.
2. Serve chicken with sauce over mashed sweet potato drizzled with tahini sauce.

Nutrition : Calories: 223; Total Fat: 8.7 g; Carbs: 0.7 g; Dietary Fiber: 0.2 g; Sugars: 0.2 g; Protein: 35.5 g; Cholesterol: 101 mg; Sodium: 214 mg

Instant Pot Coconut Curry Turkey

Yield: 4 | Total Time: 20 Mins | Prep Time: 5 Mins | Cook Time: 15 Mins

Ingredients

- 1-pound turkey
- 15 ounces water
- 30 ounces light coconut milk
- ½ cup Thai red curry sauce
- ¼ cup cilantro
- 2½ tsp. lemon garlic seasoning

Directions

1. In an instant pot, combine turkey, water, coconut milk, red curry paste, cilantro, and lemon garlic seasoning; stir to mix well and lock lid; cook on high pressure for 15 Mins and then release pressure naturally. Serve garnished with cilantro.

Nutrition : Calories: 569; Total Fat: 55.4 g; Carbs: 13.7 g; Dietary Fiber: 5.7 g; Sugars: 7.8 g; Protein: 14.2 g; Cholesterol: 0 mg; Sodium: 49 mg

Instant Pot Green Chile Chicken

Yield: 6 | Total Time: 30 Mins | Prep Time: 10 Mins | Cook Time: 20 Mins

Ingredients

- 3 pounds chicken thighs
- 3 to 4 tomatillos, husked and diced
- 1 tsp black pepper
- 1 tsp ground coriander
- 2 tsp cumin
- 1-1/2 tsp sea salt
- 3 cloves garlic, chopped finely
- 1/2-pound diced chilies
- 1 medium red onion, diced
- chopped cilantro, garnish
- Fresh lime wedges, garnish

Directions

1. Lay chicken in the bottom of your instant pot; sprinkle with spices and toss until well coated. Add garlic, green chilies, red onion and tomatillos. Lock lid and cook on high for 20 Mins and then let pressure come down naturally.
2. Remove chicken and shred with fork to serve.

Nutrition : Calories: 347; Total Fat: 12.9 g; Carbs: 4.7 g; Dietary Fiber: 0.7 g; Sugars: 1.5 g; Protein: 49.7 g; Cholesterol: 151 mg; Sodium: 496 mg

Healthy Chicken Super Salad

Yield: 1 | Total Time: 30 Mins | Prep Time: 10 Mins | Cook Time: 20 Mins

Ingredients

- 1 red onion, sliced
- 2 tbsp. extra virgin olive oil
- 1 large date, chopped
- 1 tbsp. capers
- ¼ cup rocket
- 1/4 avocado, peeled, stoned and sliced
- 150g chicken slices
- ¼ cup chicory leaves
- 2 tbsp. chopped walnuts
- 1 tbsp. fresh lemon juice
- ¼ cup chopped parsley
- ¼ cup chopped celery leaves

Directions

1. Add water to your instant pot and insert a metal trivet; season chicken with salt and pepper and place it over the trivet. Lock lid and cook on high setting for 20 Mins. Let pressure come down naturally. Arrange salad leaves in a large bowl or a plate; mix the remaining ingredients well and serve over the salad leaves.

Nutrition : Calories: 288; Fat: 19.5g; Carbs: 9.7g; Protein: 21.6g

Grilled Herb Marinade Chicken with Sautéed Mushrooms

Yield: 4 | Total Time: 40 Mins | Prep Time: 10 Mins | Cook Time: 30 Mins

Ingredients

- 1 cup chopped mixed fresh herb leaves (basil, parsley, cilantro)
- 2 large garlic cloves, chopped
- 1/4 cup apple cider vinegar
- 1/4 cup extra-virgin olive oil
- 3 teaspoons sea salt
- 1/4 teaspoon pepper
- 2 lbs. chicken breasts, boneless, skinless, sliced in half lengthwise
- 4 cups button mushrooms
- 1 1/2 tablespoons butter
- 2 red onions, chopped

Directions

1. In a food processor, process together herbs, garlic, vinegar, oil, salt and pepper until smooth; transfer to a Ziploc bag and add chicken. Shake to coat chicken well and refrigerate for about 30 Mins.
2. Set your instant pot on manual high and heat in oil; add chicken and cook for 5 Mins per side or until browned. Remove chicken and add water to the pot; insert a trivet and place the chicken over the trivet. Lock lid and cook for 30 Mins. Let pressure come down naturally.
3. Add butter to a skillet over medium heat and sauté red onion until fragrant; stir in mushrooms and cook for about 6 Mins or until tender; season with salt and pepper. Serve grilled chicken over the sautéed mushrooms.

Nutrition : Calories: 504; Fat: 34g; Carbs: 9.9g; Protein: 39.6g

Tropical Turkey Salad

Yield: 6 | Total Time: 50 Mins | Prep Time: 20 Mins | Cook Time: 30 Mins

Ingredients

- 2 cups chopped cooked turkey
- 1/2 cup chopped green onion
- 1 cup chopped orange segments
- 1 cup diced red bell pepper
- 1 cup pineapple chunks
- 1 cup diced celery
- 1 tablespoon fresh lemon juice
- 1 teaspoon liquid Stevia
- 2 tablespoons mango chutney
- 1/3 cup sour cream
- 1/4 teaspoon curry powder

Directions

1. Add water to an instant pot and insert a trivet; season turkey with salt and pepper and place over the trivet. Lock lid and cook for 30 Mins. Let pressure come down naturally.
2. In a small bowl, whisk together lemon juice, sour cream, Stevia, and curry powder until well blended; refrigerate until ready to use.
3. In a bowl, mix the turkey with the remaining ingredients; drizzle with dressing and toss until well coated. Refrigerate for at least 1 hour before serving.

Nutrition : Calories: 126; Total Fat: 3.2 g; Carbs: 9.6 g; Protein: 14.4 g; Cholesterol: 38 mg; Sodium: 46 mg

Instant Pot Grilled Chicken & Green Onion

Yield: 1 Serving | Total Time: 50 Mins | Prep Time: 10 Mins | Cook Time: 40 Mins

Ingredients

- 3 ounces chicken breast
- 1 tablespoon olive oil
- 1 green onion, chopped
- Pinch of garlic powder
- Pinch of sea salt
- Pinch of pepper
- 1 cup steamed green beans

Directions:

1. Set your instant pot on manual high and heat in oil; add chicken and cook for 5 Mins per side or until browned. Remove chicken and add water to the pot; insert a trivet. Place the chicken in aluminum foil and top with onion slices. Sprinkle with garlic powder, salt and pepper and wrap the foil; place over the trivet. Lock lid and cook for 30 Mins. Let pressure come down naturally.
2. Serve chicken over steamed green beans.

Nutrition : Calories: 176; Total Fat: 6.3 g; Carbs: 3.4 g; Dietary Fiber: 0.8 g; Sugars: 1.5 g; Protein: 5 g; Cholesterol: 76 mg; Sodium: 61 mg

Healthy Turkey Chili

Yield: 2 | Total Time: 1 Hour 10 Mins | Prep Time: 10 Mins | Cook Time: 1 Hour

Ingredients

- 1-pound lean ground turkey
- 2 tablespoons olive oil
- 1 garlic clove, minced
- 1 large red onion, chopped
- 1 (15-ounces) can black beans
- 1 (8-ounces) can tomato sauce
- 1 (28-ounces) can crushed tomatoes
- 1 green bell pepper, chopped
- 1 red bell pepper, chopped
- 1 package (1 1/4-oz.) chili seasoning mix
- 1/2 teaspoon sea salt

Directions

1. Set your instant pot on manual high, cook ground turkey, garlic and onion until turkey is no longer pink. Stir in the remaining ingredients. Lock lid and cook for 1 hour. Let pressure come down on its own. Serve hot with your favorite toppings.

Nutrition : Calories: 314; Total Fat: 19.2 g; Carbs: 13.5 g; Dietary Fiber: 9.7 g; Sugars: 3.3 g; Protein: 40 g; Cholesterol: 68 mg; Sodium: 746 mg

INSTANT POT KETO EGG RECIPES

Breakfast Meaty Quiche

Yield: 6 | Total Time: 40 Mins | Prep Time: 10 Mins | Cook Time: 30 Mins

Ingredients

- 2 cups chopped green onions
- ¼-pound diced ham
- ¼-pound ground turkey
- 4 tablespoons olive oil
- 6 slices cooked bacon, crumbled
- 1 cup milk
- 4 large eggs
- 1 cup shredded cheese
- 1/4 tsp. salt
- 1/8 tsp. pepper

Directions

1. Set your instant pot to manual high; heat oil and cook in ground turkey until browned. Mix green onions, ham, cooked turkey, bacon and cheese. Whisk together milk, eggs, salt and pepper in a large bowl until well blended and pour over the meat and stir to mix well.
2. Lock lid and cook for 30 Mins. When ready, let pressure come down on its own.
3. Remove from the pot and sprinkle with more cheese. Broil until cheese is melted and serve.

Nutrition : Calories: 394; Total Fat: 32.6g; Carbs: 4.1g; Protein: 21.3g

Breakfast Eggs de Provence

Yield: 4 | Total Time: 20 Mins | Prep Time: 10 Mins | Cooking Time: 10 Mins

Ingredients

- 1 ½ cups cream cheese
- 3 large eggs
- ½-pound cooked ham, diced
- 1 red onion, chopped
- 1 cup cheddar cheese
- 1 ½ cup chopped kale leaves
- 1 tsp Herbes de Provence
- 1/8 tsp. sea salt
- 1/8 tsp. pepper

Directions

1. In a bowl, beat cream cheese and eggs until well blended; stir in the remaining ingredients and pour the mixture into an instant pot. Lock lid and set it to manual high setting. Cook for 10 Mins and then release the pressure naturally.
2. Serve hot with a glass of fresh orange juice.

Nutrition : Calories: 585; Total Fat: 47.6g; Carbs: 7.5g; Protein: 32.5g

Instant Pot Keto Bacon-Spinach Frittata

Yield: 4 | Total Time: 37 Mins | Prep Time: 10 Mins | Cook Time: 27 Mins

Ingredients

- 2 tablespoons butter
- 8 eggs
- 1 cup fresh spinach
- 5 ounces diced bacon
- 1 cup heavy whipping cream
- salt & pepper
- ¾ cup shredded cheese

Directions

1. Set your instant pot to manual high; melt in butter and the fry bacon for about 7 Mins. Stir in spinach until wilted and remove the pan from heat; set aside.
2. In a small bowl, whisk together cream and eggs until well combined and then pour in the pot; top with spinach, bacon and cheese. Lock lid and cook for 15 Mins. When ready, let pressure come down on its own.

Nutrition : Calories: 559; Total Fat: 47.5g; Carbs: 2.6g; Protein: 30.4g

Roasted Veggie Breakfast Frittata

Yield: 8 | Total Time: 1 Hour 20 Mins | Prep Time: 30 Mins | Cook Time: 50 Mins

Ingredients

- 4 tbsp. extra virgin olive oil
- 1 cup fresh cremini mushrooms, sliced
- 20 egg whites, beaten
- 1 cup cheddar cheese
- 1/2 cup chopped fresh baby spinach
- 1 cup sweet red pepper strips
- 1 cup thin red onion wedges
- Olive oil cooking spray
- 2 tbsp. fresh oregano, snipped
- 1/4 tsp. black pepper
- 1/4 tsp. sea salt

Directions

1. Set your instant pot to manual high. Toss together extra virgin olive oil, sweet pepper, mushrooms, onion, salt and pepper in a large bowl until well combined. Spoon the mixture evenly into the pot and roast for about 20 Mins or until the veggies are tender. Toss together the roasted veggies and spinach; spread the mixture in the pot and sprinkle with pieces of cheese and pour the egg whites on top. Lock lid and cook for 30 Mins. When ready, let pressure come down on its own. Serve sprinkled with oregano.

Nutrition : Calories: 362; Total Fat: 24.1g; Carbs: 6.9g; Protein: 26.8g

Instant Pot Avocado Shrimp Omelet

Yields: 2 | Total Time: 40 Mins | Prep Time: 10 Mins | Cook Time: 30 Mins

Ingredients

- 150g shrimp, peeled and deveined
- 4 large free-range eggs, beaten
- 1 medium avocado, diced
- 1 large tomato, diced
- 2 tablespoons coconut oil
- 1/8 tsp. freshly ground black pepper
- 1/4 tsp. sea salt
- 1 tbsp. freshly chopped cilantro

Directions

1. Set your instant pot to manual high; cook shrimp until it turns pink; chop the cooked shrimp and set aside.
2. In a small bowl, toss together avocado, tomato, and cilantro; season with sea salt and pepper and set aside.
3. In a separate bowl, beat the eggs and set aside.
4. Melt coconut oil in the pot and then add in the egg mixture. Arrange the shrimp on top of the egg and lock lid; cook for 5 Mins and then let pressure come down on its own.

Nutrition : Calories: 475; Total Fat: 38.3g; Carbs: 11.8g; Protein: 25.2g

Healthy Frittata w/ Scallions & Smoked Salmon

Yield: 6 | Total Time: 30 Mins | Prep Time: 10 Mins | Cook Time: 20 Mins

Ingredients

- 2 tablespoons extra virgin olive oil
- 4 scallions, trimmed and chopped
- 3 large eggs
- 3 large egg whites
- ½ teaspoon finely chopped fresh tarragon
- ¼ cup water
- ½ teaspoon salt
- 2 ounces smoked salmon, sliced into small pieces
- 2 tablespoons black olive tapenade

Directions

1. Set your instant pot to manual high; add extra virgin olive oil and heat until hot, but not smoking; stir in scallions and sauté until fragrant. In a bowl, beat together eggs, egg whites, tarragon, water, and salt; season with black pepper and pour into the pot. Arrange the salmon onto the egg mixture. Cook, stirring frequently, for about 2 Mins or until almost set. Lock lid and cook for 14 Mins. When ready, let pressure come down on its own.
2. Remove the frittata from the pot and transfer to a serving plate; slice and serve with tapenade.

Nutrition : Calories: 102; Total Fat: 8.5g; Carbs: 1.3g; Protein: 5.1g

Instant Pot Cheesy Green Omelet

Yield: 4 | Total Time: 30 Mins | Prep Time: 10 Mins | Cook Time: 20 Mins

Ingredients

- 4 tbsp. extra virgin olive oil
- 8 large eggs
- 1 red onion, finely chopped
- 2 tsp. chopped parsley
- ½ cup cheddar cheese
- Handful rocket leaves
- Salt and pepper

Directions

1. Set your instant pot to manual high; add extra virgin olive oil and heat until hot, but not smoking; stir in the red onion and fry for about 5 Mins. Whisk the eggs well and add to the pot with the onion; evenly distribute the egg mixture and sprinkle with grated cheese. Lock lid and cook for 15 Mins and then let pressure come down on its own. Remove the omelet from the pot and sprinkle with parsley and rocket; season with salt and pepper and roll up the omelet.
2. Serve right away.

Nutrition : Calories: 345; Total Fat: 28.7g; Carbs: 4.7g; Protein: 17.1g

Instant Pot Sausage & Broccoli Quiche

Yield: 6 | Total Time: 1 Hour 10 Mins | Prep Time: 15 Mins | Cook Time: 55 Mins

Ingredients

- 4 cups broccoli
- 300g breakfast sausage
- 3 cups almond flour
- 1 tablespoon sea salt
- 8 eggs
- 2 tablespoons coconut oil
- 2 tablespoons water

Directions

1. Steam the broccoli and set aside.
2. Set your instant pot to manual high and cook the sausage until browned; set aside.
3. Blend almond flour and sea salt in a food processor until well combined; add one egg and coconut oil and continue processing to form a ball.
4. Spread the dough in the pot and top with broccoli and sausage.
5. In a bowl, whisk the remaining eggs with water and pour over the broccoli and sausage.
6. Lock lid and cook for 35 Mins. Release the pressure naturally and serve warm.

Nutrition : Calories: 391; Total Fat: 32.3g; Carbs: 9.2g; Protein: 19.6g

Instant Pot Salmon Omelet

Yield: 1 | Total Time: 25 Mins | Prep Time: 10 Mins | Cook Time: 15 Mins

Ingredients

- 1 tablespoon extra virgin olive oil
- 1 oz. sliced smoked salmon
- 2 tablespoons capers
- 1 large egg
- 10g chopped rocket
- 1 teaspoon chopped parsley
- 1 red onion, chopped

Directions

1. Beat the egg in a large bowl; stir in salmon, rocket, capers, red onion, and chopped parsley.
2. Set your instant pot to manual high; add extra virgin olive oil and heat until hot, but not smoking; add the egg mixture and spread the mixture evenly in the bottom of the pot. Lock lid and cook for 15 Mins. When ready, let pressure come down on its own.
3. With a spatula, roll the omelet in half and serve hot.

Nutrition : Calories: 275; Total Fat: 19.8g; Carbs: 11.9g; Protein: 13.4g

Low-Carb Keto Instant Pot Egg Salad

Yield: 4 | Total Time: 10 Mins | Prep Time: 5 Mins | Cook Time: 5 Mins

Ingredients

- 6 eggs
- 1 tsp. lemon juice
- 1 tsp. Dijon mustard
- 2 tbsp. mayonnaise
- 1/8 tsp. kosher salt
- 1/8 tsp. pepper
- 2 lettuce leaves to serve

Directions

1. Add water to your instant pot and insert a trivet; place eggs in a metal dish and place on a trivet; lock lid and cook on high for 5 Mins and then let pressure come down on its own.
2. Transfer the eggs to a bowl of cold water and let cool completely; peel and add to a food processor. Pulse until chopped. Add lemon juice, mustard, mayonnaise, salt and pepper and continue pulsing until smooth. Spoon the egg mixture over lettuce leaves and wrap. Serve.

Nutrition : Calories: 129; Total Fat: 9.1 g; Carbs: 2.4 g; Dietary Fiber: 0.1 g; Sugars: 1 g; Protein: 8.4 g; Cholesterol: 247 mg; Sodium: 233 mg

Instant Pot Keto Jalapeno Omelettes

Yield: 4 | Total Time: 20 Mins | Prep Time: 10 Mins | Cook Time: 10 Mins

Ingredients

- ¼ cup heavy cream
- 1 cup cheddar cheese, shredded
- 4 jalapeno peppers, chopped
- 8 slices bacon, chopped
- 12 large eggs
- ¼ tsp. sea salt
- 1/8 tsp. pepper

Directions

1. Grease jars with oil and set aside.
2. In a skillet set over medium heat, cook bacon until crispy and then set aside on a plate; add jalapenos in bacon fat and cook for about 2 Mins or until tender and then remove from fat to a plate.
3. In a bowl, whisk together heavy cream, eggs, salt and pepper and then fold in bacon, peppers and shredded cheese. Divide the egg mixture among four greased jars and place them on a trivet in an instant pot; add two cups of water and lock lid. Cook on high for 5 Mins and then let pressure come down on its own.

Nutrition : Calories: 590; Total Fat: 46.3g; Carbs: 3g; Protein: 30.4g

Instant Pot Keto Mini Mushroom Quiche

Yield: 6 | Total Time: 17 Mins | Prep Time: 7 Mins | Cook Time: 10 Mins

Ingredients

- 4 eggs
- 1/2 cup shredded Swiss cheese
- 1 scallion, chopped
- 1/4 cup heavy cream
- 2 ounces chopped cremini mushrooms
- 1/2 tsp. salt
- 1 cup water

Directions

1. Press Swiss cheese in the bottom of a silicone mold and up the sides; divide chopped mushrooms among the molds and top with chopped scallions.
2. In a blender, blend together cream, eggs and salt; pour over the mushrooms.
3. Add a cup of water to your instant pot and place on the trivet; place the silicon tray over the trivet and lock lid. Cook on high for 5 Mins and then release pressure quickly. Broil for 5 Mins in oven until lightly browned and serve.

Nutrition : Calories: 97; Total Fat: 7.3 g; Carbs: 1.4 g; Dietary Fiber: 0.1 g; Sugars: 0.6 g; Protein: 6.5 g; Cholesterol: 127 mg; Sodium: 256 mg

Keto Breakfast Casserole

Yield: 6 | Total Time: 45 Mins | Prep Time: 15 Mins | Cook Time: 30 Mins

Ingredients

- 2 tablespoons coconut oil
- 1 ⅓ cups sliced leek
- 2 teaspoons minced garlic
- 1 cup chopped kale
- 8 eggs
- ⅔ cups sweet potato, peeled and grated
- 1 ½ cups breakfast sausage

Directions

1. Set your instant pot to sauté mode and melt coconut oil; stir in garlic, leeks, and kale and sauté for about 5 Mins or until tender; transfer the veggies to a plate and clean the pot.
2. Whisk together eggs, beef sausage, sweet potato and the sautéed veggies in a large bowl until well blended; pour the mixture in a heatproof bowl or pan. Add water to the instant pot and insert a trivet; place the bowl onto the trivet and lock lid. Cook on manual for 25 Mins and then let pressure come down on its own. Remove the casserole and cut into equal slices.

Nutrition : Calories: 199; Total Fat: 13.5 g; Carbs: 9.3 g; Dietary Fiber: 0.6 g; Sugars: 2.7 g; Protein: 10.6 g; Cholesterol: 180 mg; Sodium: 277 mg

Healthy Veggie Frittata

Yields: 4 | Total Time: 30 Mins | Prep Time: 10 Mins | Cook Time: 20 Mins

Ingredients

- 8 free-range eggs, whisked
- ½ cup milk
- 2 tbsp. chopped green onions
- 2 tbsp. chopped leek
- 2 tbsp. chopped fresh chives
- 2 tbsp. chopped fresh dill
- 4 tomatoes, diced
- 1 tsp. red pepper flakes
- 2 garlic cloves, minced
- Coconut oil, for greasing the pan
- Sea salt
- Black pepper

Directions

1. Grease a cast iron skillet or saucepan and set aside.
2. In a large bowl, whisk together the eggs; beat in the remaining ingredients until well mixed.
3. Pour the egg mixture into the prepared pan and. Add water to the instant pot and insert a trivet; place the pan onto the trivet and lock lid. Cook on high for 20 Mins and then let pressure come down on its own. Remove the casserole and cut into equal slices.
4. Garnish the frittata with extra chives and dill to serve.

Nutrition : Calories: 203; Total Fat: 13.2 g; Carbs: 9.3 g; Dietary Fiber: 2 g; Sugars: 5.6 g; Protein: 13.8 g; Cholesterol: 330 mg; Sodium: 148 mg

Instant Pot Frittata with Pesto

Yield: 4 | Total Time: 60 Mins | Prep Time: 10 Mins | Cook Time: 50 Mins

Ingredients

- 4 tbsp. extra virgin olive oil
- 3 cloves garlic, minced
- 1 cup white onion, diced
- 200g ground beef
- 8 eggs, beaten
- ¼ cup basil pesto
- 200g bottled roasted red peppers, drained then sliced
- 1 cup baby arugula, torn
- ¼ tsp freshly ground black pepper
- ½ tsp kosher salt
- 1 cup shredded cheddar cheese

Directions

1. Set your instant pot to manual high and then add in olive oil; sauté the onions for about 5 Mins or until tender. Add in the garlic and sauté for 1 minute until fragrant; stir in ground beef and cook until browned; stir in eggs, arugula, red peppers, pesto, and cheese, and salt and pepper until well combined. Lock lid and cook for 40 Mins and then naturally release the pressure.
2. Enjoy!

Nutrition : Calories: 482; Total Fat: 35.4 g; Carbs: 7.8 g; Dietary fiber: 1.4 g; Sugars: 4.4 g; Protein: 34.4 g; Cholesterol: 744 mg; Sodium: 402 mg

Instant Pot Berry Omelet

Yield: 4 | Total Time: 20 Mins | Prep Time: 10 Mins | Cook Time: 10 Mins

Ingredients

- 8 eggs
- 1 cup milk
- 1 teaspoon cinnamon
- 4 tbsp. olive oil
- 1 cup grated cottage cheese
- 1 ½ cups chopped raspberries, blueberries, and strawberries

Directions

1. In a bowl, beat together the egg, milk and cinnamon until well blended.
2. Add oil to an instant pot set to manual high. Add the egg mixture and swirl to cover the base evenly. Lock lid and cook the egg mixture for 10 Mins. Let pressure come down on its own.
3. Transfer the omelet to a plate and sprinkle with cheese. Top with berries and roll up to serve.

Nutrition : Calories: 353; Total Fat: 25.4 g; Carbs: 11.7 g; Dietary Fiber: 3.3 g; Protein: 21.4 g; Cholesterol: 337 mg; Sodium: 382 mg; Sugars: 5.7 g

Instant Pot Low Carb Casserole

Yield: 6 | Total Time: 35 Mins | Prep Time: 10 Mins | Cooking Time: 25 Mins

Ingredients

- 12 large eggs
- 1 1/4 pounds diced ham
- 1 cup olive oil
- 500 grams raw radishes, sliced thinly into strips
- 1/2 cup diced red onions
- 1 clove fresh garlic, minced
- 1/2 teaspoon sea salt
- 1/4 teaspoon pepper
- 1 teaspoon seasoning
- 1 ½ cups water
- 1 cup spinach
- ½ cup chopped green bell pepper
- 1 cup parmesan cheese, grated

Directions

1. Set your instant pot to manual high setting and heat in olive oil and add onions and radishes; sprinkle with salt and pepper and cook, stirring occasionally, for about 3 Mins or until tender.
2. Whisk eggs and seasoning in a bowl until frothy and then add to the pot; stir to combine. Stir in diced ham, chopped green pepper and spinach; top with grated cheese. Lock lid and cook for 20 Mins.
3. Serve warm.

Nutrition : Calories: 489; Total Fat: 40.1g; Carbs: 7g; Protein: 25.6g

Asian Breakfast Eggs

Yield: 1 Serving | Total time: 10 Mins | Prep time: 5 Mins | Cook time: 5 Mins

Ingredients

- 1 large egg
- pinch of sesame seeds
- 1 tsp chopped scallions
- 1/3 cup cold water
- pinch of garlic powder
- pinch of salt
- pinch of pepper

Directions

1. In a small bowl, whisk together water and eggs until frothy; strain the mixture through a fine mesh into a heat proof bowl. Whisk in the remaining ingredients until well combined; set aside.
2. Add a cup of water to an instant pot and place a steamer basket or trivet in the pot; place the bowl with the mixture over the basket and lock lid. Cook on high for 5 Mins and then naturally release pressure.
3. Serve hot with a glass of freshly squeezed orange juice.

Nutrition : Calories: 76; Total Fat: 5.2 g; Carbs: 0.9 g; Dietary Fiber: 0.2 g; Sugars: 0.5 g; Protein: 6.5 g; Cholesterol: 186 mg; Sodium: 228 mg

Keto Mexican Frittata

Yield: 4 | Total Time: 35 Mins | Prep Time: 10 Mins | Cook Time: 25 Mins

Ingredients

- 1 cup half and half
- 4 eggs
- 1 cup diced green chilis
- 1 cup shredded Mexican blend cheese
- 1/4 cup chopped cilantro
- 1/2 tsp. salt
- 1/2 tsp. ground cumin

Directions

1. In a bowl, whisk together half and half, eggs, green chilis, ½ cup shredded cheese, cumin and salt until well combined; pour the mixture into a greased metal pan and cover with foil.
2. Add two cups of water in an instant pot and place on a trivet; place the pan over the trivet and lock lid; cook on high for 20 Mins and then let the pressure come down on its own.
3. Remove lid and sprinkle with the remaining cheese and cilantro; broil for about 5 Mins or until cheese is bubbly and browned.

Nutrition : Calories: 381; Total Fat: 19 g; Carbs: 11.5 g; Dietary Fiber: 0.1 g; Sugars: 5.3 g; Protein: 19.3 g; Cholesterol: 284 mg; Sodium: 1322 mg

Low Carb Instant Pot Egg Cups

Yield: 4 | Total Time: 18 Mins | Prep Time: 5 Mins | Cook Time: 13 Mins

Ingredients

- 1/4 cup half and half
- 4 eggs
- 1/2 cup shredded cheddar cheese
- 1/4 cup each of diced red onions, bell peppers, mushrooms, and tomatoes)
- 2 tbsp. chopped cilantro
- Salt & Pepper
- 1/2 cup shredded parmesan

Directions

1. In a bowl, beat together half and half, eggs, cheddar, veggies, cilantro, salt and pepper; pour in half-pint jars and cover with lids.
2. Add two cups of water to an instant pot and place in a trivet; place the jars on trivet and lock lid; cook on high pressure for 10 Mins and then quickly release the pressure.
3. Top with parmesan cheese and broil for about 3 Mins or until cheese is bubbly and lightly browned. Enjoy!

Nutrition : Calories: 240; Total Fat: 10.8 g; Carbs: 2.1 g; Dietary Fiber: 0.1 g; Sugars: 0.6 g; Protein: 9.5 g; Cholesterol: 184 mg; Sodium: 156 mg

Instant Pot Spiced Salmon Frittata

Yield: 2 | Total Time: 30 Mins | Prep Time: 10 Mins | Cook Time: 20 Mins

Ingredients:

- 1 tablespoon coconut oil
- 1 red onion, chopped
- 1 green pepper, chopped
- 2 garlic cloves, minced
- 1 ½ cups cherry tomatoes
- 1/2 teaspoon paprika
- 1 teaspoon cumin
- 1/2 cup wild-caught salmon
- 6 free-range eggs, beaten
- Pinch of sea salt
- Pinch of pepper
- 2 tablespoons chopped cilantro

Directions:

1. Set your instant pot to manual high and melt in butter; sauté red onion and green pepper; stir in garlic and cook for about 2 Mins or until fragrant. Stir in paprika, cumin, salt and pepper and cook for about 1 minute; stir in tomatoes and cook until soft. Sprinkle with salmon and cover with eggs; season with salt and pepper and lock lid. Cook on high for 15 Mins and then release the pressure naturally. Serve warm garnished with cilantro.

Nutrition : Calories: 344; Total Fat: 22 g; Carbs: 16 g; Dietary Fiber: 4.2 g; Sugars: 8.4 g; Protein: 23.5 g; Cholesterol: 500 mg; Sodium: 325 mg

Korean Steamed Breakfast Eggs

Yield: 1 | Total time: 10 Mins | Prep time: 5 Mins | Cook time: 5 Mins

Ingredients

- 1 tablespoon melted butter
- 1 large egg
- pinch of sesame seeds
- 1 tsp. chopped scallions
- 1/3 cup cold water
- pinch of garlic powder
- pinch of salt
- pinch of pepper

Directions

1. In a small bowl, whisk together butter and eggs until frothy; strain the mixture through a fine mesh into a heatproof bowl. Whisk in the remaining ingredients until well combined; set aside.
2. Add a cup of water to an instant pot and place a steamer basket or trivet in the pot; place the bowl with the mixture over the basket and lock lid. Cook on high for 5 Mins and then naturally release pressure.
3. Serve hot with a glass of freshly squeezed orange juice.

Nutrition : Calories: 76; Total Fat: 15.2 g; Carbs: 0.9 g; Dietary Fiber: 0.2 g; Sugars: 0.5 g; Protein: 6.5 g; Cholesterol: 186 mg; Sodium: 228 mg

Pressure Cooked Zucchini & Beef Frittata

Yield: 4 | Total Time: 35 Mins | Prep Time: 15 Mins | Cook Time: 20 Mins

Ingredients:

- 1 tablespoon butter
- 1/2 red onion, minced
- 1 clove garlic, minced
- 8 ounce ground beef, crumbled
- 4 zucchinis, thinly sliced
- 6 free-range eggs
- Pinch of sea salt
- Pinch of pepper

Directions:

1. Set your instant pot to manual high and melt in butter; sauté red onion for about 3 Mins or until tender; add garlic, beef, and zucchini and cook for about 7 Mins or until zucchini is tender and beef is cooked through. Season with salt and pepper and pour in the egg. Lock lid and cook on high for 10 Mins and then release the pressure naturally. Serve warm.

Nutritional Information per Serving:

Calories: 263; Total Fat: 13.3 g; Carbs: 8.6 g; Dietary Fiber: 2.5 g; Sugars: 4.5 g; Protein: 28.1 g; Cholesterol: 304 mg; Sodium: 229 mg

Instant Pot Breakfast Casserole

Yield: 6 | Total Time: 45 Mins | Prep Time: 15 Mins | Cook Time: 30 Mins

Ingredients

- 2 tbsp. coconut oil
- 1 ⅓ cups sliced leek
- 2 tsp. minced garlic
- 1 cup chopped kale
- 8 eggs
- ⅔ cups sweet potato, peeled and grated
- 1 ½ cups breakfast sausage,

Directions

1. Set your instant pot to sauté mode and heat coconut oil; stir in garlic, leeks, and kale and sauté for about 5 Mins or until tender; transfer the veggies to a plate and clean the pot.
2. Whisk together eggs, beef sausage, sweet potato and the sautéed veggies in a large bowl until well blended; pour the mixture in a heatproof bowl or pan. Add water to the instant pot and insert a trivet; place the bowl onto the trivet and lock lid. Cook on manual for 25 Mins and then let pressure come down on its own. Remove the casserole and cut into equal slices.

Nutrition : Calories: 280; Total Fat: 19 g; Carbs: 7 g; Dietary Fiber: 1 g; Sugars: 2 g; Protein: 25 g; Cholesterol: 295 mg; Sodium: 160 mg

Easy Breakfast Casserole

Yields: 5 to 6 | Total Time: 55 Mins | Prep Time: 20 Mins | Cook Time: 35 Mins

Ingredients

- 1½ pounds breakfast sausage
- 1 large yam or sweet potato, diced
- 4 tbsp. melted coconut oil
- 10 eggs, whisked
- ½ tsp. garlic powder
- 2 cups chopped spinach
- ½ yellow onion, diced
- ½ tsp. sea salt

Directions

1. Coat a 9x12 baking dish with cooking spray.
2. Toss the diced sweet potatoes in coconut oil and sprinkle with salt. Set aside.
3. Set a sauté pan over medium heat; add yellow onion and sauté for about 4 Mins or until fragrant. Stir in breakfast sausage and cook for about 5 Mins or until the sausage is no longer pink.
4. Transfer the sausage mixture to the baking dish and add spinach and sweet potatoes. Top with eggs and sprinkle with garlic powder and salt. Mix until well combined and pour the mixture in a heatproof bowl or pan. Add water to the instant pot and insert a trivet; place the dish on the trivet and lock the lid. Cook on high for 25 Mins and then let pressure come down on its own. Remove the casserole and cut into equal slices.

Nutrition : Calories: 176; Total Fat: 15.2 g; Carbs: 0.9 g; Dietary Fiber: 0.2 g; Sugars: 0.5 g; Protein: 6.5 g; Cholesterol: 186 mg; Sodium: 228 mg

Keto Mini Mushroom Quiche

Yield: 6 | Total Time: 30 Mins | Prep Time: 10 Mins | Cook Time: 20 Mins

Ingredients

- 9 eggs
- 1 cup shredded Swiss cheese
- 1 cup scallion, chopped
- 1/2 cup heavy cream
- 1 cup chopped cremini mushrooms
- 2 tbsp. olive oil
- ½ tsp. black pepper
- 1/2 tsp. salt
- 1 cup water

Directions

1. Set your instant pot to manual high and then heat olive oil; sauté scallions until fragrant and add mushrooms; cook for a few Mins and then transfer to a plate.
2. Press Swiss cheese in the bottom of the pot and up the sides; top with the cooked mushrooms and extra scallions.
3. In a blender, blend together cream, eggs, pepper and salt; pour over the mushrooms.
4. Lock lid and cook on high setting for 15 Mins. Release the pressure naturally and then broil in the oven for 5 Mins or until lightly browned.

Nutrition : Calories: 246; Total Fat: 20 g; Carbs: 3.6 g; Dietary fiber: 0.6 g; Sugars: 1.4 g; Protein: 14 g; Cholesterol: 329 mg; Sodium: 276 mg

Instant Pot Breakfast Eggs & Sausage

Yield: 6 | Total Time: 25 Mins | Prep Time: 10 Mins | Cook Time: 15 Mins

Ingredients

- 8 eggs
- 1-pound chorizo sausage, chopped
- ¼ cup Kalamata olives, pitted and coarsely chopped
- ½ cup roasted red peppers, drained and cut into long strips
- 2 tbsp. extra virgin olive oil
- ½ tsp harissa paste
- 1 tsp Stevia
- 1 tsp. salt
- ¼ cup tomato sauce
- 1 tbsp. freshly chopped parsley
- 1 cup grated parmesan cheese

Directions

1. Set your instant pot to manual high and heat olive oil; fry the sliced sausage until crispy. Stir in the tomato sauce, harissa, Stevia, salt and the roasted peppers. Simmer for 10 Mins then stir in the sliced olives.
2. Make four wells in the sausage sauce and crack the 4 eggs into each well. Lock lid and cook on high setting for 5 Mins; let pressure come down on its own.
3. Garnish with the chopped parsley and sprinkle with salt and freshly ground pepper if desired. Serve immediately with the crusty bread.
4. Enjoy!

Nutrition : Calories: 541; Total Fat: 41.1 g; Carbs: 4.4 g; Dietary Fiber: 0.5 g; Sugars: 1.6 g Protein: 31.9 g; Cholesterol: 298 mg; Sodium: 1716 mg

Green Eggs with Bacon

Yield: 6 | Total Time: 25 Mins | Prep Time: 10 Mins | Cook Time: 15 Mins

Ingredients

- 12 eggs
- 4 bacon strips, fried and crumbled
- 2 tbsp. milk
- ¼ cup Kalamata olives, pitted and chopped
- 3 tbsp. chopped roasted red peppers
- 2 cups fresh baby spinach
- 1 tbsp. extra virgin olive oil
- ¼ cup crumbled bacon
- ½ tsp kosher salt
- 1 cup crumbled feta cheese

Directions

1. Set your instant pot on manual high and heat olive oil; sauté spinach until wilted and then transfer to a plate.
2. Beat the eggs together with the milk, salt and pepper in a medium bowl.
3. Add the remaining oil to the pot and pour in egg mixture; scramble the eggs using a rubber spatula being careful not to overcook them.
4. Stir in the spinach, olives, bacon, roasted peppers and feta cheese until well combined. Lock lid and cook on high for 3 Mins. Let pressure come down.
5. Serve the green eggs with freshly squeezed orange juice.
6. Enjoy!

Nutrition : Calories: 297; Total Fat: 22.8 g; Carbs: 3.2 g; Dietary Fiber: 0.5 g; Sugars: 2.2 g Protein: 20.2 g; Cholesterol: 365 mg; Sodium: 980 mg

Instant Pot Egg Mug

Yield: 3 | Total Time: 20 Mins | Prep Time: 10 Mins | Cook Time: 10 Mins

Ingredients

- 4 large eggs
- 1 tomato, sliced
- 1 cup egg whites
- 3 fresh basil leaves
- 1 cup fresh mozzarella
- 1 tsp aged balsamic vinegar
- 2 tbsp. olive oil

Directions

1. Grease a mug with the olive oil and add all the ingredients apart from the egg, balsamic vinegar and egg whites and pop in the microwave for half a minute.
2. Crack the egg and add to the mug together with the egg whites, stirring very gently with the other ingredients.
3. Insert a metal trivet in the instant pot and add in water; place the mug over the trivet. Lock lid and cook for 10 Mins on high. Remove from the pot and drizzle with the aged balsamic vinegar.
4. Let it stand for a minute or so and serve with crusty bread.

Nutrition : Calories: 248; Total Fat: 17.8 g; Carbs: 2.2 g; Dietary Fiber: 0.3 g; Sugars: 1.6 g Protein: 20.1 g; Cholesterol: 253 mg; Sodium: 233 mg

Instant Pot Greek Breakfast Sausage

Yield: 4 | Total Time: 16 Mins | Prep Time: 10 Mins | Cook Time: 6 Mins

Ingredients

- 450g minced lamb
- 4 tbsp. olive oil
- 450g minced pork
- ¼ cup ice water
- 4 cloves garlic, minced
- ¼ tsp cayenne pepper
- 1 tsp oregano
- 1 tsp fennel seed
- 1 tbsp. kosher salt
- 1 tsp ground coriander
- Finely grated zest of 2 oranges

Directions

1. Combine the minced meats in a large bowl.
2. In a small separate bowl, combine all the spices and add them to the meat. Also add the ice water and use your hands to mix everything up.
3. Cover the bowl with plastic wrap and refrigerate for at least one hour up to overnight.
4. Divide the meat mixture into 16 portions and flatten to form rounded disks.
5. Set your instant pot to manual high and heat oil; add in the disks and lock lid. Cook for 6 Mins and then let pressure come down on its own. Transfer to a plate lined with paper towels
6. Enjoy!

Nutrition : Calories: 498; Total Fat: 26.4 g; Carbs: 1.6 g; Dietary Fiber: 0.5 g; Sugars: 0.1 g Protein: 21.4 g; Cholesterol: 183 mg; Sodium: 1895 mg

INSTANT POT VEGETARIAN AND VEGAN KETO

RECIPES

Sage-Infused Butternut Squash Zucchini Noodles

Yield: 4 | Total Time: 25 Mins | Prep Time: 10 Mins | Cook Time: 15 Mins

Ingredients

- 3 large zucchinis, spiralized or julienned into noodles
- 3 cups cubed butternut squash
- 2 cloves garlic, finely chopped
- 1 yellow onion, chopped
- 2 tablespoons olive oil
- 2 cups homemade vegetable broth
- ¼ teaspoon red pepper flakes
- Freshly ground black pepper
- 1 tablespoon fresh sage, finely chopped
- Salt, to taste and smoked salt for garnish

Directions

1. Add the oil to a pan over medium heat and sauté the sage once it's hot until it turns crisp. Transfer to a small bowl and season lightly with salt then set aside.
2. Add the onion, butternut, garlic, broth, salt and pepper flakes to in instant pot and lock the lid; cook on high pressure for 10 Mins and then release pressure naturally.
3. Meanwhile, steam the zucchini noodles in your microwave or steamer until crisp-tender.
4. Once the butternut mixture is ready, remove from heat and let cool off slightly then transfer to a blender and process until smooth.
5. Combine the zucchini noodles and the butternut puree in the skillet over medium heat and cook until heated through and evenly coated for 2 Mins.
6. Sprinkle with fried sage and smoked salt and serve hot.

Nutrition : Calories: 301; Total Fat: 28.5 g; Carbs: 13.8 g; Dietary Fiber: 3.4g; Sugars: 4.8 g; Protein: 1.9 g; Cholesterol: 0 mg; Sodium: 161 mg

Instant Pot Coconut Curry Tofu

Yield: 4 | Total Time: 20 Mins | Prep Time: 5 Mins | Cook Time: 15 Mins

Ingredients

- 1-pound tofu
- 15 ounces water
- 30 ounces light coconut milk
- ½ cup Thai red curry sauce
- ¼ cup cilantro
- 2½ tsp. lemon garlic seasoning

Directions

1. In an instant pot, combine tofu, water, coconut milk, red curry paste, cilantro, and lemon garlic seasoning; stir to mix well and lock lid; cook on high pressure for 15 Mins and then release pressure naturally. Serve garnished with cilantro.

Nutrition : Calories: 569; Total Fat: 55.4 g; Carbs: 13.7 g; Dietary Fiber: 5.7 g; Sugars: 7.8 g; Protein: 14.2 g; Cholesterol: 0 mg; Sodium: 49 mg

Asian Saag Aloo

Yield: 4-6 | Total Time: 20 Mins | Prep Time: 10 Mins | Cook Time: 10 Mins

Ingredients

- 500g fresh spinach, roughly chopped
- 200g fresh baby spinach
- 2 tbsp. ginger root, crushed
- 4 cloves garlic, crushed
- 350ml coconut milk
- ¼ cup frozen peas
- 2 pkts marinated tofu
- 1 cup tomato sauce
- 2 tbsp. tomato ketchup
- 1 tbsp. ground coriander
- 1 tbsp. ground cumin
- 1 tbsp. garam masala
- 1 pinch cayenne pepper
- 2 tbsp. cilantro, chopped
- Salt to taste

Directions

1. First, set aside the baby spinach. Combine all the remaining ingredients in your instant pot and lock lid; cook on high pressure for 10 Mins and then release the pressure naturally.
2. Use an immersion blender to puree the entire mixture. (You can omit the blending part if you don't like your food mushy). Fold in the baby spinach and cover the pot until spinach is wilted.
3. Serve hot with roast potatoes.

Nutrition : Calories: 210; Total Fat: 16.1 g; Carbs: 13.8 g; Dietary Fiber: 5.3 g; Sugars: 5.9 g; Protein: 8.2 g; Cholesterol: 0 mg; Sodium: 410 mg

Creamy Cauliflower 'Mashed Potatoes'

Yield: 4 | Total Time: 20 Mins | Prep Time: 10 Mins | Cook Time: 10 Mins

Ingredients

- 1 whole cauliflower, cut into florets
- 4 cloves garlic, peeled and roughly chopped
- 2 tbsp. butter
- 2 tbsp. cream cheese
- 1 bay leaf
- 3 cups water
- 1 cup low-fat milk
- Salt and pepper to taste

Directions

1. Combine the cauliflower florets in your instant pot with all the ingredients apart from the milk and cream cheese. Lock lid and cook on high pressure for 10 Mins. Release the pressure naturally and then discard the bay leaf and garlic cloves and drain off the water. Mash the cauliflower using a potato masher or an immersion blender if you want it very creamy. If you are adding milk, do so a tablespoon at a time, until you get the desired consistency. Blend in the coconut cream.
2. Season with salt and pepper and garnish with chopped chives or chopped green onions and serve with your favorite stew. Enjoy!

Nutrition : Calories: 242; Total Fat: 21.7 g; Carbs: 13.9 g; Dietary Fiber: 6.8 g; Sugars: 7.3 g; Protein: 5.9 g; Cholesterol: 0 mg; Sodium: 79 mg

Instant Pot Spanish Tortilla

Yield: 4 | Total Time: 25 Mins | Prep Time: 10 Mins | Cook Time: 15 Mins

Ingredients

- 6 large eggs
- 1/4 cup milk
- 1 tablespoon butter melted
- 4 oz. raw potatoes, sliced thinly into strips
- 1/4 cup diced red onions
- 1 clove fresh garlic, minced
- 1/2 teaspoon sea salt
- 1/4 teaspoon pepper
- 1 teaspoon tomato paste
- 2 tablespoons baking mix
- 1 teaspoon seasoning
- 4 oz. grated parmesan cheese
- 1 ½ cups water
- 1 cup spinach
- 1 cup chopped green bell pepper

Directions

1. Soak the potato strips in water for at least 20 Mins.
2. Whisk eggs and seasoning in a bowl until frothy.
3. In another bowl, whisk together milk, baking mix and tomato paste until well blended and then whisk into the egg mixture; stir in garlic and onion. Grease your casserole dish.
4. Drain the potato strips and dry with paper towel; add to the casserole dish and pour in the melted butter. Pour in the egg mixture, chopped green pepper and spinach; top with grated cheese. Add water to your instant pot and insert a trivet; place the casserole dish over the trivet and lock lid. Cook on high for 15 Mins and then let pressure come down on its own. Serve warm.

Nutrition : Calories: 283; Total Fat: 17.4 g; Carbs: 12.8 g; Dietary Fiber: 1.6 g; Sugars: 4 g; Protein: 20.6 g; Cholesterol: 308 mg; Sodium: 688 mg

Sage-Infused Butternut Squash Zucchini Noodles

Yield: 4 | Total Time: 25 Mins | Prep Time: 10 Mins | Cook Time: 15 Mins

Ingredients

- 3 large zucchinis, spiralized or julienned into noodles
- 3 cups cubed butternut squash
- 2 cloves garlic, finely chopped
- 1 yellow onion, chopped
- 2 tbsp. olive oil
- 2 cups homemade vegetable broth
- ¼ tsp. red pepper flakes
- Freshly ground black pepper
- 1 tbsp. fresh sage, finely chopped
- Salt, to taste and smoked salt for garnish

Directions

1. Add the oil to a pan over medium heat. Once it's hot, sauté the sage until crisp. Transfer to a small bowl, season lightly with salt, then set aside.
2. Add the onion, butternut, garlic, broth, salt, and pepper flakes to an instant pot and lock the lid; cook on high pressure for 10 Mins and then release pressure naturally.
3. Meanwhile, steam the zucchini noodles in your microwave or steamer until crisp-tender.
4. Once the butternut mixture is ready, remove from heat; let it cool off slightly, then transfer to a blender and process until smooth.
5. Combine the zucchini noodles and the butternut puree in the skillet over medium heat and cook until heated through and evenly coated for two Mins.
6. Sprinkle with fried sage and smoked salt and serve hot.

Nutrition : Calories: 301; Total Fat: 28.5 g; Carbs: 13.8 g; Dietary Fiber: 3.4g; Sugars: 4.8 g; Protein: 1.9 g; Cholesterol: 0 mg; Sodium: 161 mg

Keto Coconut Porridge

Yield: 6 | Total Time: 15 Mins | Prep Time: 5 Mins | Cook Time: 10 Mins

Ingredients

- ¼ cup almond flour
- 1/4 cup dried shredded coconut (unsweetened)
- 2 2/3 cups water
- 2 cups coconut milk
- 1/4 cup psyllium husks
- 2 tsp. liquid Stevia
- 1/4 tsp. nutmeg
- 1/2 tsp. cinnamon
- 1 tsp. vanilla extract

Directions

1. Add coconut to your instant pot and set it on sauté setting; cook, stirring until toasted; stir in water and coconut milk; lock lid and cook on high for 5 Mins and then quick release the pressure; stir in the remaining ingredients.

Nutrition : Calories: 310; Total Fat: 24.1 g; Carbs: 13.9 g; Dietary Fiber: 5.4 g; Sugars: 4.1 g; Protein: 3.9 g; Cholesterol: 0 mg; Sodium: 74 mg

Instant Pot Coconut Cabbage

Yield: 6 | Total Time: 25 Mins | Prep Time: 15 Mins | Cook Time: 10 Mins

Ingredients

- 2 tbsp. coconut oil
- 2 tbsp. olive oil
- 1/4 cup desiccated unsweetened coconut
- 2 tbsp. lemon juice
- 1 medium carrot, sliced
- 1 medium yellow onion, sliced
- 1 medium cabbage, shredded
- 1 tbsp. turmeric powder
- 1 tbsp. mild curry powder
- 1 tsp. mustard powder
- ½ long red chili, sliced
- 2 large cloves of garlic, diced
- 1½ tsp. salt
- ⅓ cup water

Directions

1. Turn your instant pot on sauté mode and add coconut oil; stir in onion and salt and cook for about four Mins. Stir in spices, chili, and garlic for about 30 seconds. Stir in the remaining ingredients and lock the lid; set on manual high for 5 Mins. When done, naturally release the pressure and stir the mixture. Serve with beans or rice.

Nutrition : Calories: 231; Total Fat: 22.5 g; Carbs: 11.9 g; Dietary Fiber: 8.5 g; Sugars: 3.7 g; Protein: 5.9 g; Cholesterol: 0 mg; Sodium: 582 mg

Yummy Brussels Sprouts

Yield: 4 | Total Time: 16 Mins | Prep Time: 10 Mins | Cook Time: 6 Mins

Ingredients

- 2 pounds Brussels sprouts, halved
- 1 tbsp. chopped almonds
- 1 tbsp. rice vinegar
- 2 tbsp. sriracha sauce
- 1/4 cup soy sauce
- 4 tbsp. sesame oil
- 1/2 tbsp. cayenne pepper
- 1 tbsp. smoked paprika
- 1 tsp. onion powder
- 2 tsp. garlic powder
- 1 tsp. red pepper flakes
- Salt and pepper

Directions

1. Set your pot to sauté and add in almond; cook for about 3 Mins and then stir in all the seasonings and liquid ingredients. Stir in Brussels sprouts and set on manual high for 3 Mins. When done, quick release pressure and serve over rice.

Nutrition : Calories: 185; Total Fat: 18.7 g; Carbs: 10.8 g; Dietary Fiber: 9.8 g; Sugars: 5.8 g; Protein: 8.8 g; Cholesterol: 0 mg; Sodium: 114 mg

Peperonata (Tasty Pepper Salad)

Yield: 4 | Total Time: 15 Mins | Prep Time: 5 Mins | Cook Time: 10 Mins

Ingredients:

- 2 red capsicums, sliced into strips
- 2 yellow capsicums, sliced into strips
- 1 green capsicum, sliced into strips
- 2 tbsp. olive oil
- 1 red onion
- 2 garlic cloves
- 3 tomatoes, chopped
- basil, chopped
- salt and pepper

Directions

1. Add oil to your instant pot and sauté onions until tender; add one garlic clove and capsicums and cook until browned. Add the chopped tomatoes, salt, and pepper and stir to mix; lock lid and cook on high pressure for 5 Mins and then release pressure naturally.
2. Press the remaining garlic clove and set aside.
3. Remove capsicums into a bowl and add olive oil, garlic and chopped basil; mix well and serve.

Nutrition : Calories: 148; Total Fat: 21.1 g; Carbs: 9.2 g; Dietary Fiber: 2.9 g; Sugars: 5.1 g; Protein: 1.8 g; Cholesterol: 0 mg; Sodium: 6 mg

Instant Pot Korean Breakfast Eggs

Yield: 1 Serving | Total time: 10 Mins | Prep time: 5 Mins | Cook time: 5 Mins

Ingredients

- 1 large egg
- pinch of sesame seeds
- 1 tsp. chopped scallions
- 1/3 cup cold water
- pinch of garlic powder
- pinch of salt
- pinch of pepper

Directions

1. In a small bowl, whisk together water and eggs until frothy; strain the mixture through a fine mesh into a heatproof bowl. Whisk in the remaining ingredients until well combined; set aside.
2. Add a cup of water to an instant pot and place a steamer basket or trivet in the pot; place the bowl with the mixture over the basket and lock lid. Cook on high for 5 Mins and then naturally release pressure.
3. Serve hot with a glass of freshly squeezed orange juice.

Nutrition : Calories: 76; Total Fat: 5.2 g; Carbs: 0.9 g; Dietary Fiber: 0.2 g; Sugars: 0.5 g; Protein: 6.5 g; Cholesterol: 186 mg; Sodium: 228 mg

Arugula, Orange & Kamut Salad

Yield: 6 | Total Time: 28 Mins | Prep Time: 10 Mins | Cook Time: 18 Mins

Ingredients

- 1 cup whole Kamut grains, rinsed
- 1 teaspoon vegetable oil
- 2 cups water
- 1 teaspoon sea salt
- ½ lemon
- ¼ cup chopped walnuts
- 3 tablespoons extra virgin olive oil
- 2 medium blood oranges, sliced
- 2 cups rocket Arugula

Directions

1. In a bowl, combine kamut grains, lemon juice and 4 cups of water; soak overnight.
2. Strain the kamut and add to an instant pot along with oil, salt and water; lock the lid and cook on high pressure for 18 Mins. Release the pressure naturally and then transfer to a serving bowl; stir in olive oil, walnuts, orange pieces and arugula. Serve right away.

Nutrition : Calories: 246; Total Fat: 18.6 g; Carbs: 11.7 g; Dietary Fiber: 2.1 g; Sugars: 0.4 g; Protein: 2.8 g; Cholesterol: 0 mg; Sodium: 43 mg

Creamy Cauliflower Mash

Yield: 4 | Total Time: 20 Mins | Prep Time: 10 Mins | Cook Time: 10 Mins

Ingredients

- 1 whole cauliflower, cut into florets
- 4 cloves garlic, peeled and roughly chopped
- 1 tbsp. coconut oil
- 2 tbsp. coconut cream
- 1 bay leaf
- 3 cups water
- 1 cup coconut milk
- Salt and pepper to taste

Directions

1. Combine the cauliflower florets in your instant pot with all the ingredients apart from the milk and cream. Lock lid and cook on high pressure for 10 Mins. Release the pressure naturally and then discard the bay leaf and garlic cloves and drain off the water. Mash the cauliflower using a potato masher or an immersion blender if you want it very creamy. If you are adding milk, do so a tablespoon at a time, until you get the desired consistency. Blend in the coconut cream.
2. Season with salt and pepper and garnish with chopped chives or chopped green onions and serve with your favorite stew. Enjoy!

Nutrition : Calories: 242; Total Fat: 19.7 g; Carbs: 13.9 g; Dietary Fiber: 6.8 g; Sugars: 7.3 g; Protein: 5.9 g; Cholesterol: 0 mg; Sodium: 79 mg

Delicious Sage-Infused Butternut Squash Zucchini Noodles

Yield: 4 | Total Time: 25 Mins | Prep Time: 10 Mins | Cook Time: 15 Mins

Ingredients

- 3 large zucchinis, spiralized or julienned into noodles
- 3 cups cubed butternut squash
- 2 cloves garlic, finely chopped
- 1 yellow onion, chopped
- 2 tablespoons olive oil
- 2 cups homemade vegetable broth
- ¼ teaspoon red pepper flakes
- Freshly ground black pepper
- 1 tablespoon fresh sage, finely chopped
- Salt, to taste and smoked salt for garnish

Directions

1. Add the oil to a pan over medium heat and sauté the sag until it turns crisp. Transfer to a small bowl and season lightly with salt then set aside.
2. Add the onion, butternut, garlic, broth, salt and pepper flakes to in instant pot and lock the lid; cook on high pressure for 10 Mins and then release pressure naturally.
3. Meanwhile, steam the zucchini noodles in your microwave or steamer until crisp-tender.
4. Once the butternut mixture is ready, remove from heat and let cool off slightly then transfer to a blender and process until smooth.
5. Combine the zucchini noodles and the butternut puree in the skillet over medium heat and cook until heated through and evenly coated for 2 Mins.
6. Sprinkle with fried sage and smoked salt and serve hot.

Nutrition : Calories: 301; Total Fat: 28.5 g; Carbs: 13.8 g; Dietary Fiber: 3.4g; Sugars: 4.8 g; Protein: 1.9 g; Cholesterol: 0 mg; Sodium: 161 mg

Tasty Coconut Cabbage

Yield: 6 | Total Time: 25 Mins | Prep Time: 15 Mins | Cook Time: 10 Mins

Ingredients

- 2 tablespoons coconut oil
- 2 tablespoons olive oil
- ½ cup desiccated unsweetened coconut
- 2 tablespoons lemon juice
- 1 medium carrot, sliced
- 1 medium brown onion, sliced
- 1 medium cabbage, shredded
- 1 tablespoon turmeric powder
- 1 tablespoon mild curry powder
- 1 teaspoon mustard powder
- ½ long red chili, sliced
- 2 large cloves of garlic, diced
- 1 + ½ teaspoons salt
- ⅓ cup water

Directions

1. Turn your instant pot on sauté mode and add coconut oil; stir in onion and salt and cook for about 4 Mins. Stir in spices, chili and garlic for about 30 seconds. Stir in the remaining ingredients and lock the lid; set on manual high for 5 Mins. When done, naturally release the pressure and stir the mixture. Serve with beans or rice.

Nutrition : Calories: 431; Total Fat: 22.5 g; Carbs: 15.9 g; Dietary Fiber: 8.5 g; Sugars: 3.7 g; Protein: 5.9 g; Cholesterol: 0 mg; Sodium: 582 mg

Instant Pot Freekeh & Roasted Cauliflower w/ Tahini Sauce

Yield: 4-6 | Total Time: 30 Mins | Prep Time: 15 Mins | Cook Time: 15 Mins

Ingredients

For the freekeh:
- 1 ¼ - 1 ½ cups cracked freekeh
- ¼ cup sliced almonds
- 2 cloves garlic, minced
- 1 tablespoon olive oil
- ¼ teaspoon coriander
- ½ teaspoon salt
- ¼ teaspoon cumin
- 3 ½ cups homemade vegetable stock

For the cauliflower:
- 1 large cauliflower, cut into florets
- 3 tablespoons olive oil
- Black pepper and salt to taste

Tahini sauce:
- 1/3 cup tahini
- 2 cloves garlic, minced
- 3 tablespoons freshly squeezed lime juice
- 1/3 cup water
- A large pinch of red pepper flakes
- Black pepper and salt to taste

Toppings:
- Sesame seeds
- Chopped cilantro
- Raisins

Directions

1. Preheat your oven to 425 degrees F. Arrange the cauliflower on a baking sheet and toss with salt, pepper and olive oil. Spread them in one layer and roast for half an hour, until they start turning golden, turning them halfway through cook time.
2. Meanwhile, add a tablespoon of olive oil to an instant pot set on sauté mode and cook the almonds for 3 Mins or until they start browning. Toss in the freekeh and cook for 2 Mins then add the remaining dry ingredients and cook for a minute. Add broth, salt and pepper and lock the lid; cook on high pressure for 10 Mins and then release the pressure naturally. Remove from heat and fluff with a fork. Whisk the dressing ingredients until smooth then set aside. To serve, start with the freekeh followed by the roasted cauliflower and top with the tahini sauce. Garnish with the desired toppings and serve immediately.

Nutrition : Calories: 278; Total Fat: 27.8 g; Carbs: 6.6 g; Dietary Fiber: 2.7g; Sugars: 0 g; Protein: 4.9g; Cholesterol: 0 mg; Sodium: 321 mg

Yummy Refried Beans

Yield: 6 | Total Time: 35 Mins | Prep Time: 5 Mins | Cook Time: 30 Mins

Ingredients

- 4 tablespoons olive oil
- 2 pounds dried pinto beans, sorted and soaked, rinsed
- 5 garlic cloves, roughly chopped
- 1 1/2 cups chopped onion
- 3 tablespoons vegetable shortening
- 1 1/2 teaspoons ground cumin
- 2 teaspoons dried oregano
- 1 jalapeno, seeded and chopped
- 4 cups vegetable broth
- 1-2 teaspoons sea salt
- 4 cups water
- 1/2 teaspoon ground black pepper

Directions

1. Mix all the ingredients in an instant pot and lock the lid; press the chili or bean button for 30 Mins. When done, let pressure release naturally.
2. Stir in sea salt and transfer the mixture to a blender; blend to your desired consistency and serve.

Nutrition : Calories: 303; Total Fat: 21.6 g; Carbs: 12.3 g; Dietary Fiber: 2.8 g; Sugars: 8.1 g; Protein: 5.9 g; Cholesterol: 0 mg; Sodium: 413 mg

Pressure Cooked Navy Beans, Split Pea & Sweet Potatoes Bowl

Yield: 4-6 | Total Time: 40 Mins | Prep Time: 10 Mins | Cook Time: 30 Mins

Ingredients

- 3 tablespoons coconut oil
- ½ cup dried navy beans
- 1 cup split peas
- 1 medium sweet potato, diced
- 1/2 cup nutritional yeast
- ½ teaspoon liquid smoke
- bay leaves
- Pinch of pepper
- Pinch of sea salt
- 5 cups water

Directions

1. In an instant pot, mix coconut oil, navy beans, split peas, sweet potatoes, water and liquid smoke; cook on high pressure for 20 Mins. Naturally release pressure and stir in salt, pepper and nutritional yeast. Serve.

Nutrition : Calories: 263; Total Fat: 20.6 g; Carbs: 11.3 g; Dietary Fiber: 3.4 g; Sugars: 5.5 g; Protein: 1.2 g; Cholesterol: 0 mg; Sodium: 411 mg

Healthy Italian Mushrooms

Yield: 4 | Total Time: 25 Mins | Prep Time: 10 Mins | Cook Time: 15 Mins

Ingredients

- 1-pound Portobello mushrooms, cleaned and sliced
- 2 tbsp. garlic infused ghee
- 1 ½ cups grated Parmesan cheese
- 1 ½ cups chopped tomatoes
- 1 tsp. dried oregano
- 1 tbsp. chopped fresh parsley
- 2 tbsp. chopped fresh basil
- salt and pepper

Directions:

1. Add water to your instant pot and insert a trivet.
2. In a nonstick pan set over medium heat, heat garlic infused ghee; stir in mushrooms, salt and pepper and cook for about 5 Mins.
3. Remove the pan from heat and transfer the cooked mushrooms to a baking pan.
4. In a bowl, mix canned tomatoes, parsley, basil and herbs; season with salt and pour the mixture over the mushrooms. Top with grated cheese and place the pan over the trivet; lock lid and cook on manual for 10 Mins. Quick release pressure and let cool for a few Mins before serving.

Nutrition : Calories: 128; Total Fat: 9.1 g; Carbs: 7.1 g; Dietary Fiber: 2.2 g; Sugars: 3.8 g; Protein: 7.7 g; Cholesterol: 24 mg; Sodium: 104 mg

Instant Pot Low Carb Veggie Dish

Yield: 4 | Total Time: 15 Mins | Prep Time: 5 Mins | Cook Time: 10 Mins

Ingredients

- 1.5 cups dry Soy Curls
- 2 tsp. minced ginger
- 6 cloves garlic, minced
- 2 cups diced tomatoes
- 1 tsp. paprika
- ½ tsp. cayenne pepper
- 1 tsp. turmeric
- 1 tsp. ground cumin
- 1 tsp. graham masala
- 4 ounces heavy cream
- 4 ounces butter
- ¼-1/2 cup chopped cilantro
- 1 tsp. salt
- 1 cup water

Directions

1. In your instant pot, combine soy curls, tomatoes, spices and water and lock lid; cook on high for 6 Mins; let pressure come down on its own and then turn the pot on sauté mode and then add in cream and butter; stir until melted and crush the tomatoes with a spoon.
2. Stir in cilantro and more graham masala and serve right away.

Nutrition : Calories: 334; Total Fat: 34 g; Carbs: 7.5 g; Dietary Fiber: 1.8 g; Sugars: 2.6 g; Protein: 2.2 g; Cholesterol: 100 mg; Sodium: 764 mg

Instant Pot Keto Ham & Greens

Yield: 4 | Total Time: 14 Mins | Prep Time: 10 Mins | Cook Time: 4 Mins

Ingredients

- 2 cups tofu chopped
- 6 cloves garlic, chopped
- 1 red onion, chopped
- 8 cups chopped collard greens
- 1 tsp. dried thyme
- 2 bay leaves
- 1 tsp red pepper flakes
- ½ tsp. Salt
- ½ tsp. Pepper
- ¼ cups water
- 1 tsp. liquid smoke
- 2 tsp. hot sauce
- 1 tbsp. apple cider vinegar

Directions

1. Combine all ingredients, except liquid smoke, apple cider vinegar and hot sauce, in your instant pot; cook on high for 4 Mins and then let pressure come down on its own. Stir in hot sauce, liquid smoke and apple cider vinegar. Serve.

Nutrition : Calories: 135; Total Fat: 6.1 g; Carbs: 11.8g; Dietary Fiber: 5.1 g; Sugars: 2.1 g; Protein: 13 g; Cholesterol: 0 mg; Sodium: 387 mg

Mixed Veggie Pot Pie

Yield: 1 9-inch pie | Total Time: 1 Hour 20 Mins | Prep Time: 20 Mins | Cook Time: 1 Hour

Ingredients

For the pie crust:
- ¾ cup coconut flour
- 2 eggs
- ½ cup salted butter, chilled

For the pie filling:
- ½ cup frozen spinach, separated
- 2 cups, cauliflower florets, cut into smaller chunks
- 1/3 cup frozen peas
- ¼ cup win sauce
- ½ cup cheddar cheese, shredded

Directions

1. Add water to your instant pot and insert a trivet.
2. Prepare the pie crust as in the crusty spinach pie recipe and spread it on a 9-inch pie pan.
3. Add the cauliflower to an oven proof pan and roast until they start browning for 30 Mins.
4. Combine the roast cauliflower with the peas. Spinach, win sauce. and cheese in a mixing bowl.
5. Spread the filling on the crust and place the pan on the trivet; lock lid and cook on manual for 20 Mins. Release pressure naturally.
6. Remove from pot and let stand for 5 Mins before serving.

Nutrition : Calories: 302; Total Fat: 26.1 g; Carbs: 9.8g; Dietary Fiber: 5.1 g; Sugars: 3.3 g; Protein: 19.2 g; Cholesterol: 94 mg; Sodium: 220 mg

Instant Pot Pepper Salad

Yield: 4 | Total Time: 15 Mins | Prep Time: 5 Mins | Cook Time: 10 Mins

Ingredients:

- 2 red capsicums, sliced into strips
- 2 yellow capsicums, sliced into strips
- 1 green capsicum, sliced into strips
- ½ teaspoon olive oil
- 1 red onion
- 2 garlic cloves
- 3 tomatoes, chopped
- basil, chopped
- salt and pepper

Directions

1. Add oil to your instant pot and sauté onions until tender; add 1 garlic clove, and capsicums and cook until browned. Add the chopped tomatoes, salt and pepper and stir to mix; lock lid and cook on high pressure for 5 Mins and then release pressure naturally.
2. Press the remaining garlic clove and set aside.
3. Remove capsicums to a bowl and add olive oil, garlic and chopped basil; mix well and serve.

Nutrition : Calories: 291; Total Fat: 18.2 g; Carbs: 10.9g; Dietary Fiber: 6.9 g; Sugars: 2.2 g; Protein: 2.1 g; Cholesterol: 0 mg; Sodium: 221 mg

Egg- Sauerkraut Salad

Yield: 3-4 | Total Time: 20 Mins | Prep Time: 10 Mins | Cook Time: 10 Mins

Ingredients

- 6 eggs
- ½ - ¾ cup sauerkraut
- ¼ cup mayonnaise
- Freshly ground pepper to taste

Directions

1. In your instant pot, boil the eggs for 10 Mins.
2. Add the sauerkraut to a bowl and peel the hardboiled eggs and chop them up finely in the bowl. Add in the sauerkraut and mayonnaise and combine well until evenly mixed.
3. Season with pepper and salt and serve.
4. Enjoy!

Nutrition : Calories: 213; Total Fat: 7.9 g; Carbs: 3.6g; Dietary Fiber: 2.1 g; Sugars: 1.1 g; Protein: 22.8g; Cholesterol: 102 mg; Sodium: 212 mg

Broccoli & Cauliflower Mash

Yield: 4 | Total Time: 15 Mins | Prep Time: 10 Mins | Cook Time: 5 Mins

Ingredients

- 4 cups broccoli and cauliflower florets
- 2 tsp butter
- 3 cloves garlic
- ½ tsp freshly ground pepper
- ½ tsp salt

Directions

1. Melt the butter in your instant pot and sauté the broccoli and cauliflower. Sprinkle with salt and lock lid; cook on high for 1 minute and then quick release the pressure. Turn your pot on sauté mode and cook until the veggies lose all of their water to give them a roasty finish.
2. Combine the cooked veggies with garlic and pepper in your food processor and process until you get a mashed potato texture.
3. Serve with more butter, if desired.
4. Serve immediately.

Nutrition : Calories: 187; Total Fat: 13.8 g; Carbs: 5.8g; Dietary Fiber: 4.2 g; Sugars: 1.3 g; Protein: 3.9 g; Cholesterol: 11 mg; Sodium: 299 mg

Cheese & Broccoli Casserole

Yield: 3-4 | Total Time: 25 Mins | Prep Time: 15 Mins | Cook Time: 10 Mins

Ingredients

- 3 cups frozen broccoli
- 1 cup almond milk
- ½ cup shredded cheddar cheese
- 8 eggs
- Freshly ground pepper and salt to taste

Directions

1. Add two cups of water to your instant pot and insert a trivet.
2. Grease a large pie dish or casserole dish.
3. Combine all ingredients in a bowl, reserving a little cheese for topping.
4. Scoop into the prepared dish and top with the reserved cheese.
5. Place the dish on the trivet and lock lid; cook on manual for 5 Mins and then quick release pressure. Transfer the dish to the oven and bake for about 5 Mins or until top is browned.
6. Enjoy!

Nutrition : Calories: 296; Total Fat: 19.6 g; Carbs: 12.2g; Dietary Fiber: 5.7 g; Sugars: 5.3 g; Protein: 21.9 g; Cholesterol: 211 mg; Sodium: 493 mg

Keto Gluten-Free Coconut Breakfast Cereal

Yield: 5 | Total Time: 10 Mins | Prep Time: 5 Mins | Cook Time: 5 Mins

Ingredients

- 1 cup golden flax meal
- 1 cup coconut flour
- 1 cup coconut milk
- 2 tbsp. butter
- 4 large eggs, beaten
- 1 cup water
- ¼ tsp. salt
- 1 tbsp. liquid Stevia

Directions

1. Add in flax meal, coconut flour, water and salt to your instant pot; lock lid and cook on manual for 5 Mins; quick release pressure and then set it on sauté mode; beat in beaten egg, one at a time, until the mixture is thick. Whisk in coconut milk, butter and sweetener and then serve.

Nutrition : Calories: 334; Total Fat: 25.4 g; Carbs: 14.2g; Dietary Fiber: 8.6 g; Sugars: 1.8 g; Protein: 11.8 g; Cholesterol: 134 mg; Sodium: 178 mg

Low Carb Oatmeal

Yield: 4 | Total Time: 15 Mins | Prep Time: 5 Mins | Cook Time: 10 Mins

Ingredients

- 1/3 cup flaked coconut
- 1/3 cup flaked almonds
- 1/4 cup chia Seeds
- 1/2 cup coconut milk
- 1/4 cup shredded coconut
- 1 tsp. vanilla Extract
- 1 tsp. liquid Stevia
- 1 cup water

Directions

1. Set your instant pot on sauté mode and toast flaked almonds and coconut for about 5 Mins; add in the remaining ingredients and lock lid; cook on high for 5 Mins and then quick release the pressure.

Nutrition : Calories: 228; Total Fat: 19.4 g; Carbs: 11.2g; Dietary Fiber: 7.6 g; Sugars: 2.2 g; Protein: 5.1 g; Cholesterol: 0 mg; Sodium: 11 mg

Tasty Keto Spiced Pecans

Yield: 6 | Total Time: 25 Mins | Prep Time: 10 Mins | Cook Time: 15 Mins

Ingredients

- 3 cups raw pecans
- 1/8 tsp. cayenne pepper
- 1/8 tsp. ground ginger
- 1/2 tsp. ground nutmeg
- 1 tsp. ground cinnamon
- 1/8 tsp. sea salt
- 1 tbsp. water

Directions

1. Combine all ingredients in your instant pot and lock lid; cook on manual for 10 Mins and then quick release the pressure.
2. Transfer the mixture to a baking sheet and spread it out; bake at 350 degrees for about 5 Mins.

Nutrition : Calories per serve: 412; Fat: 35.7g; Protein: 4.58g; Carbs: 24.91g

Crusty Spinach Pie

Yield: 4 | Total Time: 30 Mins | Prep Time: 10 Mins | Cook Time: 20 Mins

Ingredients

For the pie crust:
- ¾ cup almond flour
- 4 eggs
- 3/4 cup butter

For the pie filling:
- ½ cup marinated artichoke hearts, chopped
- 1 cup frozen spinach, thawed and thoroughly drained
- 1 cup feta, crumbled
- dash of pepper

Directions

1. Add water to your instant pot and insert a trivet.
2. Combine the drained spinach and artichoke hearts and drain any present liquid then set aside.
3. Combine the almond flour and butter using a fork until you get a coarse texture. Mix in the eggs until you get a nice and thick dough. If, however the dough is too dry, add a tablespoon or two of cold water and continue kneading.
4. Press the dough into a 9-inch pie pan. Add the feta and pepper to the spinach and artichokes and toss well to combine.
5. Spread over the pie crust and place the pan on the trivet; lock lid and cook on manual for 20 Mins. Release pressure naturally.
6. Remove from pot and let stand for 5 Mins then serve.

Nutritional Info per Serving:

Calories: 591; Total Fat: 55.8g; Carbs: 9.5g; Protein: 17.1g

INSTANT POT KETO SOUPS

Instant Pot Turkey & Coconut Soup

Yield: 2 | Total Time: 40 Mins | Prep Time: 10 Mins | Cook Time: 30 Mins

Ingredients

- 1 tsp. coconut oil
- 1 red onion, finely sliced
- 1 ginger, finely chopped
- 1 clove garlic, finely chopped
- 1 lemon grass, bashed with a rolling pin
- 2 sticks celery, diced
- 1/4 cup coconut milk
- ½ cup vegetable stock
- 8 oz. turkey, cooked, roughly chopped
- 1/8 tsp. sea salt
- 1/8 tsp. black pepper
- 1 cup coriander, finely chopped
- 1 cup spinach, roughly chopped
- 2 tbsp. fresh lime juice

Directions

1. Add coconut oil to your instant pot and set it on sauté mode; stir in red onions and sauté for about 5 Mins or until translucent. Add ginger and garlic and sauté for about 3 Mins or until garlic is golden.
2. Stir in lemon grass, celery, coconut milk, vegetable sock, turkey, salt and pepper and then lock lid. Cook on high for 15 Mins and then quick release the pressure. Stir in spinach and coriander and serve into soup bowls and sprinkle with a squeeze of lime juice and coriander.

Nutrition : Calories: 327; Total Fat: 15.4 g; Carbs: 11.2 g; Dietary Fiber: 3.4 g; Sugars: 4.4 g; Protein: 35.8 g; Cholesterol: 86 mg; Sodium: 276 mg

Instant Pot Detox Veggie Soup

Yield: 1 Serving | Total Time: 15 Mins | Prep Time: 5 Mins | Cook Time: 10 Mins

Ingredients

- 1 medium cauliflower
- 8 cups water
- 1 tsp. lemon juice
- 3 tsp. ground flax seeds
- 3 cups spinach
- 1 tsp. cayenne pepper
- 1 tsp. black pepper
- 1 tsp. soy sauce

Directions:

1. Core cauliflower and cut the florets into large pieces; reserve stems for juicing.
2. Add cauliflower to an instant pot and add water; lock lid and cook on high pressure for 10 Mins. Release pressure naturally and then transfer the cauliflower to a blender along with 2 cups of cooking liquid; blend until very smooth. Add the remaining ingredients and continue blending until very smooth. Serve hot or warm.

Nutrition : Calories: 198; Total Fat: 11.2 g; Carbs: 11.1 g; Dietary Fiber: 6.3 g; Sugars: 2.9 g; Protein: 1.8 g; Cholesterol: 0 mg; Sodium: 213 mg

Instant Pot Spicy Green Soup

Yield: 2 | Total Time: 30 Mins | Prep Time: 15 Mins | Cook Time: 15 Mins

Ingredients

- 2 tablespoons olive oil
- 5 cups water
- 1 cup chickpeas
- 1 green bell pepper, chopped
- 1 red onion, chopped
- 4 celery stalks, chopped
- 2 cups chopped spinach
- 1 tsp. dried mint
- 1/2 tsp. ground cumin
- 1/2 tsp. ground ginger
- 1/2 tsp. cardamom
- 2 cloves of garlic
- 1 tbsp. coconut milk
- Pinch of sea salt
- pinch of pepper

Directions:

1. Combine all ingredients, except spinach and coconut milk, in your instant pot and lock lid; cook on high pressure for 15 Mins and then release the pressure naturally. Stir in spinach; let sit for about 5 Mins and then blend the mixture until very smooth.
2. Serve the soup in soup bowls and add coconut milk. Season with salt and more pepper and enjoy!

Nutrition : Calories: 317; Total Fat:1 2.8 g; Carbs: 11.2 g; Dietary Fiber: 6.3 g; Sugars: 4 g; Protein: 12.3 g; Cholesterol: 0 mg; Sodium: 356 mg

Instant Pot Easy Everyday Chicken Soup

Yield: 3 | Total Time: 1 Hour 10 Mins | Prep Time: 10 Mins | Cook Time: 1 Hour

Ingredients:

- 3 skinned, bone-in chicken breasts
- 6 skinned and boned chicken thighs
- 1 tsp salt
- ½ tsp freshly ground pepper
- ½ tsp chicken spice seasoning
- 3-4 carrots sliced
- 4 celery ribs, sliced
- 1 sweet onion, chopped
- 2 cans evaporated milk
- 2 cups chicken stock

1. **Directions**

   Prepare Chicken: Rub chicken pieces with salt, pepper, and chicken spice seasoning. Place breasts in an instant pot, top with thighs.
   Add carrots and next 3 ingredients. Whisk evaporated milk and stock until smooth. Pour soup mixture over vegetables. Lock lid and cook on high for 1 hour. Let pressure come down on its own. Remove chicken; cool 10 Mins. Debone and shred chicken. Stir chicken into soup-and-vegetable mixture. Cook on manual high for 1 hour before serving.

Nutrition : Calories: 282; Total Fat: 18g; Carbs: 5.6g; Protein: 24g

Comforting Chicken Soup w/ Avocado

Yield: 2 | Total Time: 40 Mins | Prep Time: 10 Mins | Cook Time: 30 Mins

Ingredients

- 200g boneless skinless chicken breast, cooked
- 3 ounces coarsely chopped celery
- 3 cloves garlic
- 1 ½ cups vegetable broth
- 1 tablespoon onion, dehydrated
- ½ teaspoon parsley
- ½ teaspoon basil
- White pepper
- Sea salt
- 1 avocado, for serving

Directions:

1. In a food processor, combine all ingredients and process until chunky. Set your instant pot on manual high and add the mixture. Lock lid and cook on high for 30 Mins. Let pressure come down on its own. Serve the soup topped with diced avocado.

Nutrition : Calories: 372; Total Fat: 31.94g; Carbs: 11.2g; Protein: 28.43g

Creamy Instant Pot Chicken & Tomato Soup

Yield: 4 | Total Time: 1 Hour 10 Mins | Prep Time: 10 Mins | Cook Time: 1 Hour

Ingredients:

- 8 frozen skinless boneless chicken breasts
- 2 tbsp. Italian Seasoning
- 1 tbsp. dried basil
- 2 cloves garlic, minced
- 1 large onion, chopped
- 2 cups coconut milk (full fat) to avoid separation
- 2 cans diced tomatoes and juice
- 2 cups chicken stock
- 1 small can of tomato paste
- sea salt & pepper

Directions

1. Put all the above ingredients into the instant pot and cook on high setting for 1 hour. Let pressure come down on its own.
   Shred the chicken, cover the pot until ready to serve.

Nutrition : Calories: 227; Total Fat: 3.8g; Carbs: 6.4g; Protein: 30g

Instant Pot Flat-Belly Soup

Yield: 4 | Total Time: 34 Mins | Prep Time: 15 Mins | Cook Time: 19 Mins

Ingredients

- 2 tbsp. extra virgin olive oil
- 1 red onion, sliced
- 2 jalapeño peppers, seeds removed and diced
- 4 cups sliced green cabbage
- 1 carrot, peeled and chopped
- 4 cups crushed tomatoes
- 2 cups diced tempeh
- 4 cups vegetable broth
- 3 tbsp. apple cider vinegar
- 2 tbsp. brown sugar
- ½ tsp. salt
- ¼ tsp. black pepper

Directions

1. Heat extra virgin olive oil in an instant pot set on sauté mode and stir in red onion, jalapenos, cabbage, and carrot; sauté for about 7 Mins or until almost tender.
2. Stir in tomatoes, tempeh, broth, apple cider vinegar, and brown sugar, salt and pepper until well combined. Lock lid and cook on high pressure for 12 Mins. Let pressure come down naturally. Serve hot.

Nutrition : Calories: 222; Total Fat: 19.7 g; Carbs: 13.7 g; Dietary Fiber: 5.9 g; Sugars: 6.3 g; Protein: 18.9 g; Cholesterol: 0 mg; Sodium: 112 mg

Instant Pot Tomato Basil Soup

Yield: 6 | Total Time: 40 Mins | Prep Time: 10 Mins | Cook Time: 20 Mins

Ingredients

- 2 cloves fresh garlic
- 4 cups tomato puree
- 2 cups vegetable broth
- ¼ cup coconut oil
- ¼ cup coconut cream
- ½ cup fresh basil leaves
- pinch of Stevia, if desired
- 1 teaspoon sea salt

Directions

1. Blend together garlic and tomatoes in a blender until very smooth; pour into your instant pot and add broth, coconut oil and salt. Lock lid and cook on high pressure for 20 Mins. When done, release pressure naturally and then stir in chopped basil and coconut cream. Blend the mixture with an immersion blender until smooth and then serve. Enjoy!

Nutrition : Calories: 327; Total Fat: 21.3 g; Carbs: 13.7 g; Dietary Fiber: 5.5 g; Sugars: 13.1 g; Protein: 15 g; Cholesterol: 0 mg; Sodium: 618 mg

Instant Pot Seafood Soup

Yield: 3 | Total Time: 1 Hour 40 Mins | Prep Time: 10 Mins | Cook Time: 1 Hour 30 Mins

Ingredients:

- 12 slices bacon, chopped
- 2 cloves garlic, minced
- 6 cups chicken stock
- 3 stalks celery, diced
- 2 large carrots, diced
- ground black pepper to taste
- ½ teaspoon red pepper flakes
- 2 cups onions
- 2 cup uncooked prawns, peeled and deveined
- 500g white fish fillet, cut into bite-size pieces
- 1 can evaporated milk

Directions

1. Set your instant pot to manual high; fry bacon in coconut oil or olive oil, add onion and garlic.
2. Pour chicken stock into the pot and stir celery, and carrots into the stock. Season with black pepper and red pepper flakes. Lock lid and cook on high for 1 hour. Let pressure come down naturally. Stir prawns and fish into the soup and cook 30 Mins on manual high. Stir evaporated milk into chowder, heat thoroughly, and serve.

Nutrition : Calories: 281; Total Fat: 9.5g; Carbs: 7.8g; Protein: 39g

Tasty Mushroom Coconut Milk Soup

Yield: 4 | Total Time: 20 Mins | Prep Time: 10 Mins | Cook Time: 10 Mins

Ingredients

- 1 ½ pounds mushrooms, trimmed
- 2 tablespoons olive oil
- 1 clove garlic, minced
- 2 red onions, chopped
- 4 cups vegetable stock
- 1 cup coconut milk
- 1 tablespoon fresh thyme
- 1/8 teaspoon sea salt
- Thyme sprigs
- 1/8 teaspoon pepper

Directions

1. Grill the mushrooms, turning frequently, for about 5 Mins or until charred and tender; set aside.
2. In an instant pot, sauté red onion in oil. Stir in vegetable stock and cook for a few Mins. Add the remaining ingredients and lock the lid; cook on high pressure for 3 Mins and then release the pressure naturally. Transfer the mixture to a blender and blend until very smooth. Serve garnished with thyme sprigs.

Nutrition : Calories: 338; Total Fat: 29.2 g; Carbs: 18.1 g; Dietary Fiber: 5.8 g; Sugars: 9.3 g; Protein: 8.8 g; Cholesterol: 0 mg; Sodium: 89 mg

Tasty Mushroom Coconut Milk Soup

Yield: 6 | Total Time: 20 Mins | Prep Time: 10 Mins | Cook Time: 10 Mins

Ingredients

- 1 ½ pounds mushrooms, trimmed
- 1 clove garlic, minced
- 2 red onions, chopped
- 4 cups vegetable stock
- 1 ½ cups coconut milk
- 1 tbsp. fresh thyme
- 1/8 tsp. sea salt
- Thyme sprigs
- 1/8 tsp. pepper

Directions

1. Grill the mushrooms, turning frequently, for about five Mins or until charred and tender; set aside.
2. In an instant pot, sauté red onion in a splash of water. Stir in vegetable stock and cook for a few Mins. Add the remaining ingredients and lock the lid; cook on high pressure for three Mins and then release the pressure naturally. Transfer the mixture to a blender and blend until very smooth. Serve garnished with thyme sprigs.

Nutrition : Calories: 338; Total Fat: 29.2 g; Carbs: 11.1 g; Dietary Fiber: 5.8 g; Sugars: 9.3 g; Protein: 8.8 g; Cholesterol: 0 mg; Sodium: 89 mg

Instant Pot Detox Veggie Soup

Yield: 1 Serving | Total Time: 15 Mins | Prep Time: 5 Mins | Cook Time: 10 Mins

Ingredients

- 1 tablespoon olive oil
- 1 medium cauliflower
- 8 cups water
- 1 tsp. lemon juice
- 3 tsp. ground flax seeds
- 3 cups spinach
- 1 tsp. cayenne pepper
- 1 tsp. black pepper
- 1 tsp. soy sauce

Directions:

1. Core cauliflower and cut the florets into large pieces; reserve stems for juicing.
2. Add cauliflower to an instant pot and add water; lock lid and cook on high pressure for 10 Mins. Release pressure naturally and transfer the cauliflower to a blender along with two cups of cooking liquid; blend until very smooth. Add the remaining ingredients and continue blending until very smooth. Serve hot or warm.

Nutrition : Calories: 198; Total Fat: 11.2 g; Carbs: 11.1 g; Dietary Fiber: 6.3 g; Sugars: 2.9 g; Protein: 1.8 g; Cholesterol: 0 mg; Sodium: 213 mg

Instant Pot Spicy Green Soup

Yield: 2 | Total Time: 30 Mins | Prep Time: 15 Mins | Cook Time: 15 Mins

Ingredients

- 5 cups water
- 1 cup chickpeas
- 1 green bell pepper, chopped
- 1 red onion, chopped
- 4 celery stalks, chopped
- 2 cups chopped spinach
- 1 tsp. dried mint
- 1/2 tsp. ground cumin
- 1/2 tsp. ground ginger
- 1/2 tsp. cardamom
- 2 cloves of garlic
- 1 tbsp. coconut milk
- 2 tablespoons olive oil
- Pinch of sea salt
- pinch of pepper

Directions:

1. Combine all ingredients, except spinach and coconut milk, in your instant pot and lock lid; cook on high pressure for 15 Mins and then release the pressure naturally. Stir in spinach; let sit for about 5 Mins and then blend the mixture until very smooth.
2. Serve the soup in soup bowls and add coconut milk. Drizzle with olive oil and season with salt and more pepper and enjoy!

Nutrition : Calories: 317; Total Fat: 18.8 g; Carbs: 11.2 g; Dietary Fiber: 6.3 g; Sugars: 4 g; Protein: 12.3 g; Cholesterol: 0 mg; Sodium: 356 mg

Lemony Veggie Soup w/ Cayenne

Yield: 4 | Total Time: 40 Mins | Prep Time: 15 Mins | Cook Time: 25 Mins

Ingredients

- 1-pound curly kale, torn
- 12 ounces baby spinach
- ¼ cup brown Arborio rice, rinsed
- 2 yellow onions, chopped
- 4 tablespoons olive oil
- 3 cups plus 2 tablespoons water
- 4 cups homemade vegetable broth
- 1 tablespoon fresh lemon juice
- 1 large pinch of cayenne pepper
- Salt, to taste

Directions

1. Add the two tablespoons of olive oil in a large pan and cook the onions over medium heat. Sprinkle with salt and cook for 5 Mins until they start browning.
2. Lower the heat and pour in two tablespoons of water. Cover and lower the heat and cook for 25 Mins until the onions caramelize, stirring frequently.
3. Meanwhile, add the remaining water, broth, and some salt to an instant pot and stir in the rice. Lock the lid and cook on high pressure for 5 Mins. Naturally release the pressure and then stir in kale, onions, spinach and cayenne and lock the lid. Let sit for about 5 Mins.
4. Use an immersion blender to puree the rice mixture until smooth then stir in the lemon juice. Serve in soup bowls and drizzle each with some olive oil.

Nutrition : Calories: 102; Total Fat: 17.4 g; Carbs: 8.3g; Dietary Fiber: 3.1g; Sugars: 2.8 g; Protein: 3.1 g; Cholesterol: 0 mg; Sodium: 109 mg

Mushroom Coconut Soup

Yield: 4 | Total Time: 20 Mins | Prep Time: 10 Mins | Cook Time: 10 Mins

Ingredients

- 1 ½ pounds mushrooms, trimmed
- 1 clove garlic, minced
- 2 red onions, chopped
- 4 cups vegetable stock
- 2 cups coconut milk
- 1 tbsp. fresh thyme
- 1/8 tsp. sea salt
- Thyme sprigs
- 1/8 tsp. pepper

Directions

1. Grill the mushrooms, turning frequently, for about five Mins or until charred and tender; set aside.
2. In an instant pot, sauté red onion in a splash of water. Stir in vegetable stock and cook for a few Mins. Add the remaining ingredients and lock the lid; cook on high pressure for three Mins and then release the pressure naturally. Transfer the mixture to a blender and blend until very smooth. Serve garnished with thyme sprigs.

Nutrition : Calories: 338; Total Fat: 29.2 g; Carbs: 18.1 g; Dietary Fiber: 5.8 g; Sugars: 9.3 g; Protein: 8.8 g; Cholesterol: 0 mg; Sodium: 89 mg

Instant Pot Black Bean Chipotle Soup

Yield:6 | Total Time: 28 Mins | Prep Time: 10 Mins | Cook Time: 18 Mins

Ingredients:

- 4 tbsp. extra virgin olive oil
- 2 medium red onions, diced
- 1 red bell pepper, diced
- 1 green bell pepper, diced
- 4 tsp. ground cumin
- 4 garlic cloves, minced
- 16 ounces dried black beans
- 7 cups hot water
- 1 tbsp. chopped chipotle chilies
- 2 tsp. coarse kosher salt
- 2 tsp. fresh lime juice
- 1/4 tsp. ground black pepper
- Optional toppings: coconut cream and avocado

Directions:

1. In a large skillet set over medium high heat, heat olive oil until hot but not smoky; sauté bell peppers and onion for about 8 Mins or until brown. Stir in cumin and garlic for about 1 minute; transfer the mixture to your instant pot and then stir in 7 cups water, chipotles and beans and lock lid; cook on high pressure for 10 Mins and then release the pressure naturally.
2. Transfer about 4 cups of the mixture to a blender and blend until very smooth; return the puree to the pot and stir in salt, lime juice and pepper until well combined. Ladle the soup into serving bowls and top with coconut cream and avocado.

Nutrition : Calories: 321; Total Fat: 23.9 g; Carbs: 17.8 g; Dietary Fiber: 9.1 g; Sugars: 7.2 g; Protein: 19.1 g; Cholesterol: 0 mg; Sodium: 309 mg

Instant Pot Spicy Coconut Cauliflower Soup

Yield: 4 | Total Time: 24 Mins | Prep Time: 10 Mins | Cook Time: 14 Mins

Ingredients

- 1 ⅓ tablespoons olive oil
- 2 cups diced cauliflower
- ⅔ cups diced carrot
- 1 cup diced red onion
- ⅛ teaspoons dried thyme
- 1 ⅓ tablespoons curry powder
- 2 ⅔ cups vegetable broth
- ⅛ teaspoons salt
- ⅛ teaspoons pepper

Directions

1. Heat oil in your instant pot and sauté red onion, cauliflower and carrots for 4 Mins; stir in spices and stock and lock lid. Cook on manual for 10 Mins and then let pressure come down naturally. Stir in coconut milk and then blend with an immersion blender until smooth. Serve topped with toasted cashews.

Nutrition : Calories: 318; Total Fat: 27 g; Carbs: 15 g; Dietary Fiber: 4 g; Sugars: 5 g; Protein: 5 g; Cholesterol: 0 mg; Sodium: 182 mg

Farmhouse Veggie Soup

Yield: 4 | Total Time: 25 Mins | Prep Time: 10 Mins | Cook Time: 15 Mins

Ingredients

- 3 tablespoon olive oil
- 1 cup dried porcini mushrooms
- 6 large button mushrooms, sliced
- 1 cup chopped kale leaves
- 1 brown onion, diced
- 4 cloves garlic, diced
- 2 medium carrots, diced
- 2 celery sticks, sliced
- 1 cup tinned chopped tomatoes
- 1 small zucchini, diced
- ½ long red chili, sliced
- ¼ teaspoon of salt
- 1 bay leaf
- 4 cups vegetable
- Chopped parsley and lemon zest for garnish

Directions

1. Turn your instant pot on sauté mode and heat coconut oil; sauté onion, carrots, celery for about 2 Mins; stir in salt. Add dried porcini mushrooms, garlic, mushrooms, and chili and cook for about 2 Mins. Stir in zucchini, kale, stock, tomatoes, and bay leaves. Press the cancel button and lock the lid and set to manual high for 10 Mins.
2. When done, let pressure release naturally and then serve in serving bowls garnished with chopped parsley and lemon zest.

Nutrition : Calories: 167; Total Fat: 21.2 g; Carbs: 8.9 g; Dietary Fiber: 2.3 g; Sugars: 3.4 g; Protein: 2.9 g; Cholesterol: 0 mg; Sodium: 85 mg

Hot Instant Pot Vegetable Soup

Yield: 4-6 | Total Time: 45 Mins | Prep Time: 15 Mins | Cook Time: 30 Mins

Ingredients

- 1 pound curly kale, torn
- 12 ounces baby spinach
- ¼ cup brown Arborio rice, rinsed
- 2 yellow onions, chopped
- 4 tablespoons olive oil
- 3 cups plus 2 tablespoons water
- 4 cups homemade vegetable broth
- 1 tablespoon fresh lemon juice
- 1 large pinch of cayenne pepper
- Salt, to taste

Directions

1. Add the two tablespoons of olive oil in a large pan and cook the onions over medium heat. Sprinkle with salt and cook for 5 Mins until they start browning.
2. Lower the heat and pour in two tablespoons of water. Cover and lower the heat and cook for 25 Mins until the onions caramelize, stirring frequently.
3. Meanwhile, add the remaining water, broth, and some salt to an instant pot and stir in the rice. Lock the lid and cook on high pressure for 5 Mins. Naturally release the pressure and then stir in kale, onions, spinach and cayenne and lock the lid. Let sit for about 5 Mins.
4. Use an immersion blender to puree the rice mixture until smooth then stir in the lemon juice. Serve in soup bowls and drizzle each with some olive oil.

Nutrition : Calories: 202; Total Fat: 17.4 g; Carbs: 8.3g; Dietary Fiber: 3.1g; Sugars: 2.8 g; Protein: 3.1 g; Cholesterol: 0 mg; Sodium: 109 mg

Chicken Enchilada Soup

Yield: 6 | Total Time: 30 Mins | Prep Time: 10 Mins | Cook Time: 20 Mins

Ingredients

- 1 ½ pounds chicken thighs, boneless, skinless
- 3 cloves garlic, minced
- 1 bell pepper, thinly sliced
- 1 onion, thinly sliced
- 1 can roasted crushed tomatoes
- 1/2 cup water

For garnish:

- fresh cilantro

- 2 cups bone broth
- 1/2 tsp smoked paprika
- 1 tsp oregano
- 1 tbsp. chili powder
- 1 tbsp. cumin
- 1/2 tsp sea salt
- 1/2 tsp pepper

- 1 avocado

Directions

1. Combine all ingredients in your instant pot, except garnishes; lock lid and cook on high pressure for 20 Mins. Release pressure naturally and shred the chicken with fork. Serve in soup bowls garnished with cilantro and avocado.

Nutrition : Calories: 313; Total Fat: 15.5 g; Carbs: 8.9 g; Dietary Fiber: 3.9 g; Sugars: 2.6 g; Protein: 34.4 g; Cholesterol: 101 mg; Sodium: 290 mg

Mushroom Coconut Soup

Yield: 4 | Total Time: 20 Mins | Prep Time: 10 Mins | Cook Time: 10 Mins

Ingredients

- 1 ½ pounds mushrooms, trimmed
- 1 clove garlic, minced
- 2 red onions, chopped
- 4 cups vegetable stock
- 2 cups coconut milk
- 1 tbsp. fresh thyme
- 1/8 tsp. sea salt
- Thyme sprigs
- 1/8 tsp. pepper

Directions

1. Grill the mushrooms, turning frequently, for about five Mins or until charred and tender; set aside.
2. In an instant pot, sauté red onion in a splash of water. Stir in vegetable stock and cook for a few Mins. Add the remaining ingredients and lock the lid; cook on high pressure for three Mins and then release the pressure naturally. Transfer the mixture to a blender and blend until very smooth. Serve garnished with thyme sprigs.

Nutrition : Calories: 338; Total Fat: 29.2 g; Carbs: 18.1 g; Dietary Fiber: 5.8 g; Sugars: 9.3 g; Protein: 8.8 g; Cholesterol: 0 mg; Sodium: 89 mg

Instant Pot Spicy Green Soup

Yield: 2 | Total Time: 30 Mins | Prep Time: 15 Mins | Cook Time: 15 Mins

Ingredients

- 2 tablespoons olive oil
- 5 cups water
- 1 cup chickpeas
- 1 green bell pepper, chopped
- 1 red onion, chopped
- 4 celery stalks, chopped
- 2 cups chopped spinach
- 1 tsp. dried mint
- 1/2 tsp. ground cumin
- 1/2 tsp. ground ginger
- 1/2 tsp. cardamom
- 2 cloves of garlic
- 1 tbsp. coconut milk
- Pinch of sea salt
- pinch of pepper

Directions:

1. Combine all ingredients, except spinach and coconut milk, in your instant pot and lock lid; cook on high pressure for 15 Mins and then release the pressure naturally. Stir in spinach; let sit for about 5 Mins and then blend the mixture until very smooth.
2. Serve the soup into soup bowls and add coconut milk. Season with salt and more pepper and enjoy!

Nutrition : Calories: 317; Total Fat: 22.8 g; Carbs: 11.2 g; Dietary Fiber: 6.3 g; Sugars: 4 g; Protein: 12.3 g; Cholesterol: 0 mg; Sodium: 356 mg

Yummy Minestrone Soup

Yield: 2 | Total Time: 1 Hour 15 Mins | Prep Time: 15 Mins | Cook Time: 1 Hour

Ingredients

- 2 Italian chicken sausage links, sliced
- 2 cups low-sodium chicken stock
- 1 cup canned navy beans, rinsed
- 2 celery stalks, sliced
- 2 carrots, sliced
- 1 onion, diced
- 1 cup canned diced tomatoes
- 2 zucchinis, sliced
- 1/2 cup pasta
- 1/2 tsp. dried thyme
- 1/2 tsp. dried sage
- 2 bay leaves
- 1/4 cup grated Parmesan
- Salt

Directions

1. Set your instant pot to manual high, stir together onions, tomatoes, beans, celery, carrots, sausage, stock, sage, thyme, and bay leaves; lock lid and cook on high for 30 Mins. Let pressure come down naturally.
2. Stir in zucchini and orzo and cook on manual high for 30 Mins. Season with sea salt and divide the soup among 8 serving bowls, discard bay leaves and top each serving with a tablespoon of grated Parmesan cheese. Enjoy!

Nutrition : Calories: 387; Total Fat: 19.8 g; Carbs: 11.8g; Dietary Fiber: 5.1 g; Sugars: 4.9 g; Protein: 21.2 g; Cholesterol: 126 mg; Sodium: 1223 mg

Instant Pot French Onion Soup

Yield: 2 | Total Time: 1 Hour 20 Mins | Prep Time: 10 Mins | Cook Time: 1 Hour 10 Mins

Ingredients:

- 4 cups organic beef broth
- 1 large red onion, thinly sliced
- 1/2 tsp. garlic powder
- 2 tbsp. Worcestershire Sauce
- 4 tbsp. grated Parmesan cheese
- 2 packets Stevia
- 1/2 tsp. dried thyme
- sea salt & pepper
- 4 slices thin Swiss cheese

Directions

1. Set your instant pot to manual high and heat oil; cook in onion until caramelized and then stir in 1 cup beef broth and garlic powder. Stir in the remaining ingredients; cook on high for 1 hour. Let pressure come down naturally. Ladle the soup into an ovenproof bowl and stir in Swiss cheese; place in a preheated oven at 150°F and cook for about 5 Mins or until cheese is melted.

Nutrition : Calories: 210; Total Fat: 12.2 g; Carbs: 7.3 g; Dietary Fiber: 0.8 g; Sugars: 3.5 g; Protein: 17.4 g; Cholesterol: 36 mg; Sodium: 991 mg

Pressure Cooked Vegetable Soup

Yield: 2 Serving | Total Time: 1 Hour 10 Mins | Prep Time: 10 Mins | Cook Time: 1 Hour

Ingredients

- 1 head cauliflower
- 8 cups water
- 1 tsp. lemon juice
- 3 tsp. ground flax seeds
- 2 cups spinach
- 1 tsp. cayenne pepper
- 1 tsp. black pepper
- 1 tsp. soy sauce

Directions:

1. Core cauliflower and cut the florets into large pieces; reserve stems for juicing.
2. Add cauliflower to a slow cooker and add water; cook on low for about 3 hours.
3. Transfer the cauliflower to a blender along with 2 cups of cooking liquid; blend until very smooth. Add the remaining ingredients and continue blending until very smooth. Serve hot or warm.

Nutrition : Calories: 135; Total Fat: 2.1 g; Carbs: 9.6g; Dietary Fiber: 6.5 g; Sugars: 2.1 g; Protein: 3.4 g; Cholesterol: 0 mg; Sodium: 223 mg

Healthy Keto Hot & Sour Soup

Yield: 6 | Total Time: 1 Hour 15 Mins | Prep Time: 15 Mins | Cook Time: 60 Mins

Ingredients

- 1 pound curly kale, torn
- 12 ounces baby spinach
- 1 pound ground turkey
- 2 yellow onions, chopped
- 2 tablespoons olive oil
- 3 cups plus 2 tablespoons water
- 4 cups homemade vegetable broth
- 1 tablespoon fresh lemon juice
- 1 large pinch of cayenne pepper
- Salt, to taste
- 2 avocados, diced, to serve
- 1 cup chopped toasted almonds to serve

Directions

1. Add the two tablespoons of olive oil in a large pan and cook the onions over medium heat. Sprinkle with salt and cook for 5 Mins until they start browning.
2. Lower the heat and pour in two tablespoons of water. Cover and lower the heat and cook for 25 Mins until the onions caramelize, stirring frequently.
3. Meanwhile, add the remaining water, broth, and some salt to an instant pot and stir in the turkey. Lock the lid and cook on high pressure for 5 Mins. Naturally release the pressure and the stir in kale, onions, spinach and cayenne and lock the lid. Let sit for about 5 Mins.
4. Serve in soup bowls and topped with avocado and toasted almonds. Enjoy!

Nutrition : Calories: 489; Total Fat: 36.7g; Protein: 25.8g; Carbs: 21.59g

Creamy Chicken Soup with Sautéed Cauliflower Rice

Yield: 1 Serving | Total Time: 45 Mins | Prep Time: 10 Mins | Cook Time: 35 Mins

Ingredients

- 1 tablespoon olive oil
- 1 red onion
- 150g boneless skinless chicken breast, cooked
- ¼ cup coarsely chopped celery
- 2 cloves garlic
- 1 ½ cups vegetable broth
- 1 tablespoon onion, dehydrated
- ½ teaspoon parsley
- ½ teaspoon basil
- White pepper
- Sea salt
- 1 cup riced cauliflower
- 2 tablespoon butter
- 1 red onion

Directions

1. Prepare cauliflower by melting butter in a skillet and then sautéing red onion. Stir in cauliflower and cook for about 4 Mins or until tender. Set aside until ready to serve.
2. In a food processor, combine the remaining ingredients, except oil and onion and process until chunky. Heat oil in your instant pot set over manual high; sauté onion until fragrant and then add the mixture. Lock lid and cook on high for 30 Mins and then let pressure come down on its own. Serve soup with creamy cauliflower.

Nutrition : Calories: 237; Fat: 18.4g; Carbs: 5.4g; Protein: 23.6g

Instant Pot Spiced Turkey Soup

Yield: 2 | Total Time: 40 Mins | Prep Time: 10 Mins | Cook Time: 30 Mins

Ingredients

- 6 ounces ground turkey, cooked
- 2 (15-ounce) can crushed or skewed tomatoes
- 3 cloves garlic, crushed
- 2 teaspoons red wine vinegar
- Pinch of parsley
- Pinch of cumin
- Pinch of basil
- Pinch of rosemary
- Pinch of red pepper flakes
- 2 cups steamed broccoli to serve

Directions:

1. Set your instant pot on manual high, add in vinegar, tomatoes, and seasonings; cook for 5 Mins and then stir in ground turkey; lock lid and cook on high for 30 Mins and then let pressure come down on its own. Serve warm over steamed broccoli.

Nutrition : Calories: 251; Fat: 20.3g; Carbs: 14.3g; Protein: 27.3g

Instant Pot Cream of Carrot Soup

Yield: 4 | Total Time: 1 Hour 25 Mins | Prep Time: 10 Mins | Cook Time: 1 Hour 15 Mins

Ingredients:

- 1 onion, diced
- 2 stalks celery, diced
- 1 large sweet potato, diced
- 8 whole carrots, sliced
- 1 liter chicken broth stock
- 1 whole bay leaf
- salt and pepper, to taste
- 4 dashes tabasco (or other hot sauce)
- 1 cup heavy cream
- 1 teaspoon parsley

Directions

1. Add all ingredients (except heavy cream and parsley) to an instant pot. Cook on high setting for 1 hour and the let pressure come down on its own. Remove bay leaf. Using a hand blender, puree the vegetables. (You may also puree in batches using a standard blender.) Set instant pot on manual high and stir in heavy cream and parsley. Check seasoning and adjust to taste. Cook for an additional 15 Mins to allow heavy cream to heat thoroughly.

Nutrition : Calories: 356: Fat: 31.7g; Carbs: 14.7g; Protein: 5g

Instant Pot Broccoli & Blue Cheese Soup

Yield: 3 | Total Time: 2 Hours 20 Mins | Prep Time: 10 Mins | Cook Time: 2 Hours

Ingredients:

- 2 red onions, diced
- 4 stick celery, sliced
- 4 leeks, sliced (white part only)
- 2 tbsp. butter
- 1 liter chicken stock
- 2 large heads of broccoli, cut into florets
- 140g (1 1/4 cups) crumbled blue cheese
- 125ml cream

Directions

1. Combine all ingredients in an instant pot; lock lid and cook on stew setting for 2 hours. Let pressure come down on its own. Using a hand blender, blitz the soup until smooth. Ladle into bowls and top with extra crumbles of blue cheese (if desired).

Nutrition : Calories: 174: Fat: 10g; Carbs: 12.8g; Protein: 7.5g

Italian Meatball Zoodle Soup

Yield: 4 | Total Time: 1 Hour 50 Mins | Prep Time: 10 Mins | Cook Time: 1 Hour 40 Mins

Ingredients:

- 8 cups beef stock
- 1 medium zucchini – spiralled
- 2 ribs celery – chopped
- 1 small onion – dice
- 1 carrot – chopped
- 1 medium tomato – diced
- 1 ½ tsp. garlic salt
- 1 ½ lb. ground beef
- ½ cup parmesan cheese – shredded
- 6 cloves garlic – minced
- 1 egg
- 4 tbs. fresh parsley – chopped
- 1 ½ tsp. sea salt
- 1 ½ tsp. onion powder
- 1 tsp. Italian seasoning
- 1 tsp. dried oregano
- ½ tsp. black pepper

Directions

1. Set your instant pot on manual high; mix in beef stock, zucchini, celery, onion, carrot, tomato, and garlic salt. Cook until veggies are tender.
2. In a large mixing bowl, combine ground beef, Parmesan, garlic, egg, parsley, sea salt, onion powder, oregano, Italian seasoning, and pepper. Mix until all ingredients are well incorporated. Form into approximately 30 meatballs. Heat olive oil in a large skillet over medium-high heat. Once the pan is hot, add meatballs and brown on all sides. No need to worry about cooking them all the way through as they will be going into the instant pot. Add meatballs to the pot and lock lid. Cook on high for 1 ½ hours. Let pressure come down on its own.

Nutrition : Calories: 352: Fat: 19g; Carbs: 4.5g; Protein: 40g

Instant Pot Indian Curried Vegetable Soup

Yield: 4 | Total Time: 1 Hour 10 Mins | Prep Time: 10 Mins | Cook Time: 1 Hour

Ingredients:

- 1 head cauliflower
- 2 cups chicken stock
- 3 cloves garlic
- 1 can coconut milk
- 1 cup plain yogurt
- 1 tablespoon curry powder
- salt and pepper to taste
- 1/4 cup roasted pine nuts
- 3/4 teaspoon garam masala
- 1/2 cup xylitol
- 1/2 tsp salt
- 1 tbsp. water

Directions

1. Cut cauliflower from stalk, place in an instant pot and add in chicken stock and garlic. Lock lid and cook on high for 1 hour.
2. Quick release the pressure and stir in coconut milk and yogurt and cook on manual high for an additional hour. Using a hand blender, blend until pureed. Sprinkle with toasted pine nuts and some fresh mint.

Nutrition : Calories: 219: Fat: 7g; Carbs: 4.1g; Protein: 33.7g

Three- Ingredient Instant Pot Veggie Beef Soup

Yield: 2 | Total Time: 40 Mins | Prep Time: 10 Mins | Cook Time: 30 Mins

Ingredients:

- 500g ground beef mince
- 500ml tomato-vegetable juice cocktail
- 2 packages frozen mixed vegetables

Directions

1. Place ground beef mince in your instant pot; cook on manual high until browned. Stir in juice cocktail and mixed vegetables. Lock lid and cook on high for 30 Mins and then let pressure come down on its own.

Nutrition : Calories: 251: Fat: 12g; Carbs: 13.5g; Protein: 21.3g

Low Carb Italian Gnocchi Soup

Yield: 3 | Total Time: 40 Mins | Prep Time: 10 Mins | Cook Time: 30 Mins

Ingredients:

- 500g ground spicy Italian sausage
- 1 small onion, diced
- 2 cloves garlic, minced
- 4 cups chicken stock or bone broth
- 1 red medium pepper, diced
- 1 cup chopped fresh or frozen spinach
- ½ cup heavy cream
- sea salt and black pepper
- optional garnish: Parmesan cheese, crumbled bacon

Directions

1. Set your instant pot on manual high; fry sausage, onion and garlic until the sausage is completely browned; stir occasionally and break up the sausage with a spoon. Add in the bone broth or chicken stock and diced red peppers and lock lid. Cook on high for 30 Mins and then let pressure come down naturally. Stir in spinach and cook on manual high for an additional 5 Mins. Stir in gnocchi & cream and season to taste with salt and pepper.

Nutrition : Calories: 336: Fat: 17g; Carbs: 4.6g; Protein: 40g

Instant Pot Keto Bolognese Mince Soup

Yield: 6 | Total Time: 1 Hour 15 Mins | Prep Time: 10 Mins | Cook Time: 1 Hour 5 Mins

Ingredients:

- 1kg beef mince
- 2 brown onions, diced
- 4 cloves garlic, crushed
- 1 cup tomato paste
- 2 tbsp. chicken stock powder or 2 Knorr Jelly pots
- 1 tin tomato soup
- 1 thin diced tomato
- 1/4 cup sweet chili sauce
- 1 tbsp. oregano
- 2 bay leaves
- 2 cups water
- 1 cup finely grated carrot
- 3-4 finely chopped sticks of celery
- 2 cups finely chopped mushrooms

Directions

1. In an instant pot, add the olive oil and set on manual high. Brown the beef and add the onions and garlic. Cook for 2 Mins more. Mix the tomato paste into the pot and cook for another 2 Mins. Mix in the remaining ingredients and lock lid. Cook on high for 1 hour and then release the pressure naturally.

Nutrition : Calories: 187: Fat: 5.2g; Carbs: 8g; Protein: 27g

Low Carb Curried Vegetable Soup

Yield: 2 | Total Time: 20 Mins | Prep Time: 10 Mins | Cook Time: 10 Mins

Ingredients:

- 1 tablespoon olive oil
- 1 medium spring onion
- 1 cup cauliflower, steamed
- 1 cup beef stock
- 125ml coconut milk
- 10 cashew nuts
- ½ teaspoon coriander
- ½ teaspoon turmeric
- ½ teaspoon cumin
- 2 tablespoons fresh parsley, finely chopped
- salt and pepper, to taste

Directions

1. Place the cauliflower and onion in an instant pot and add chicken stock. Stir in coriander, turmeric, cumin and a pinch of salt. Lock lid and cook high for 10 Mins. Quick release the pressure. Using a hand blender, puree the ingredients in the pot until smooth. Stir in the
2. coconut milk. Serve with roasted cashew nuts and top with parsley.

Nutrition : Calories: 258: Fat: 12.6g; Carbs: 10.8g; Protein: 27g

Smoky Pork Cassoulet Soup

Yield: 4 | Total Time: 2 Hour 15 Mins | Prep Time: 10 Mins | Cook Time: 2 Hours 5 Mins

Ingredients:

- 1 pack bacon, fried and crumbled
- 2 cups chopped onion
- 1 tsp dried thyme
- 1/2 tsp dried rosemary
- 3 garlic cloves, crushed
- 1/2 teaspoon salt
- 1/2 teaspoon freshly ground black pepper
- 2 cans diced tomatoes, drained
- 500g boneless pork loin roast, cut into 2cm cubes
- 250g smoked sausage, cut into 1cm cubes
- 8 teaspoons finely shredded fresh Parmesan cheese
- 8 teaspoons chopped fresh flat-leaf parsley

Directions

1. Set your instant pot on manual high and fry bacon, onion, thyme, rosemary, and garlic, then
2. add salt, pepper, and tomatoes. Add in the remaining ingredients and cook on high for 2 hours. Let the pressure come down on its own. Sprinkle with Parmesan cheese and parsley when cooked

Nutrition : Calories: 258: Fat: 12.6g; Carbs: 10.8g; Protein: 27g

South African Cabbage & Boerewors Soup

Yield: 3 | Total Time: 1 Hour 40 Mins | Prep Time: 10 Mins | Cook Time: 1 Hour 30 Mins

Ingredients:

- 2 cups sweet potatoes, cubed and peeled
- 4 cups cabbage and carrot coleslaw mix
- 1 large onion, chopped
- 500g boerewors cooked, halved lengthwise and cut into thick slices
- 4 cups chicken stock

1. **Directions**
   Place potatoes, coleslaw mix, onion, caraway seeds and sausage in an instant pot. Pour stock in pot and cook on high for 1 1/2 hours. Let pressure come down naturally.

Nutrition : Calories: 329: Fat: 12.4g; Carbs: 12g; Protein: 40g

INSTANT POT KETO STEWS

Instant Pot Spiced Coconut Fish Stew

Yield: 4 | Total Time: 35 Mins | Prep Time: 5 Mins | Cook Time: 30 Mins

Ingredients

- 1 1/2 lb. fish fillets
- 1 cup coconut milk
- 2 tbsp. coconut oil
- 1 cup onion chopped
- 1 tbsp. garlic
- 1 tbsp. ginger
- 1/2 serrano or jalapeno
- 1 cup tomato chopped
- 1 tsp ground coriander
- 1/4 tsp ground cumin
- 1/2 tsp turmeric
- 1 tsp lime juice
- 1/2 tsp black pepper and salt

Directions

1. Set your instant pot on sauté mode; heat in oil and cook onion, garlic and ginger until fragrant. Add in fish and cook for 5 Mins per side or until browned and then stir in the remaining ingredients. Lock lid. Cook on meat/stew setting for 20 Mins and then let pressure come down on its own.

Nutrition : Calories: 190; Total Fat: 11.5 g; Carbs: 6 g; Dietary Fiber: 2 g; Sugars: 3 g; Protein: 16g; Cholesterol: 33 mg; Sodium: 458 mg

Instant Pot Chicken and Vegetable Stew

Yield: 4-6 | Total Time: 45 Mins | Prep Time: 15 Mins | Cook Time: 30 Mins

Ingredients

- 4 tablespoons olive oil
- 2 red onions, chopped
- 1 pound diced chicken
- 1 pound curly kale, torn
- 12 ounces baby spinach
- 3 cups plus 2 tablespoons water
- 4 cups homemade vegetable broth
- 1 tablespoon fresh lemon juice
- 1 large pinch of cayenne pepper
- Salt, to taste

Directions

1. In an instant pot, heat oil on sauté setting and then sauté onion and salt until fragrant. Add in diced chicken and cook for 5 Mins or until browned. Stir in the remaining ingredients; lock lid and cook on high pressure for 20 Mins. Release pressure naturally.

Nutrition : Calories: 202; Total Fat: 17.4 g; Carbs: 8.3g; Dietary Fiber: 3.1g; Sugars: 2.8 g; Protein: 3.1 g; Cholesterol: 0 mg; Sodium: 109 mg

Ground Beef and Vegetable Stew

Yield: 6 | Total Time: 40 Mins | Prep Time: 10 Mins | Cook Time: 30 Mins

Ingredients

- 2 tablespoons olive oil
- 1 ½ pounds ground beef
- 1 onion, thinly sliced
- 3 cloves garlic, minced
- 1 bell pepper, thinly sliced
- 1 can roasted crushed tomatoes
- 1/2 cup water
- 2 cups bone broth
- 1/2 tsp smoked paprika
- 1 tsp oregano
- 1 tbsp. chili powder
- 1 tbsp. cumin
- 1/2 tsp sea salt
- 1/2 tsp pepper

Directions

1. In an instant pot, heat oil on sauté setting and then sauté onion and garlic until fragrant. Add in beef and cook for 5 Mins or until browned. Stir in the remaining ingredients; lock lid and cook on high pressure for 20 Mins. Release pressure naturally.

Nutrition : Calories: 313; Total Fat: 15.5 g; Carbs: 8.9 g; Dietary Fiber: 3.9 g; Sugars: 2.6 g; Protein: 34.4 g; Cholesterol: 101 mg; Sodium: 290 mg

Instant Pot Spiced and Creamy Vegetable Stew with Cashews

Yield: 4 | Total Time: 29 Mins | Prep Time: 10 Mins | Cook Time: 19 Mins

Ingredients

- 2 tablespoons olive oil
- 1 cup diced red onion
- ⅔ cups diced carrot
- 2 cups diced cauliflower
- ⅛ teaspoons dried thyme
- 1 ⅓ tablespoons curry powder
- 2 ⅔ cups vegetable broth
- ½ cup coconut cream
- ⅛ teaspoons salt
- ⅛ teaspoons pepper
- Toasted cashews for serving

Directions

1. Heat oil in your instant pot and sauté red onion, cauliflower and carrots for 4 Mins; stir in spices and stock and lock lid. Cook on manual for 10 Mins and then let pressure come down naturally. Stir in coconut cream and cook on manual high for 5 Mins. Serve the stew topped with toasted cashews.

Nutrition : Calories: 318; Total Fat: 27 g; Carbs: 15 g; Dietary Fiber: 4 g; Sugars: 5 g; Protein: 5 g; Cholesterol: 0 mg; Sodium: 182 mg

Coconut Fish Stew with Spinach

Yield: 2 | Total Time: 25 Mins | Prep Time: 5 Mins | Cook Time: 20 Mins

Ingredients

- 300g firm white fish, cubed
- 450g spinach, roughly chopped
- 100g coconut cream
- 2 ½ tbsp. Thai curry paste
- 2 tbsp. coconut oil
- 100ml water
- Kosher salt and pepper, to taste

Directions

1. Add the oil to an instant pot set on manual high. Stir in the curry paste and cook for 3 Mins to bring the spices to life.
2. Pour in the coconut cream and water and bring the sauce to a boil.
3. Add in the fish cubes and lock lid. Cook on high for 15 Mins and then let pressure come down on its own. Gently stir in the spinach and cook for 3 Mins until it wilts.
4. Serve hot!

Nutrition : Calories: 550; Total Fat: 49.5 g; Carbs: 15.9g; Protein: 20.3g

Filling Herbed Turkey Stew

Yield: 2 | Total Time: 35 Mins | Prep Time: 10 Mins | Cook Time: 25 Mins

Ingredients

- 6 ounces ground turkey, cooked
- 2 (15-ounce) can crushed or skewed tomatoes
- 3 cloves garlic, crushed
- 2 teaspoons red wine vinegar
- Pinch of parsley
- Pinch of cumin
- Pinch of basil
- Pinch of rosemary
- Pinch of red pepper flakes
- 1 Avocado for serving

Directions:

1. Set your instant pot on manual high, add in vinegar, tomatoes, and seasonings; cook for about 5 Mins. Stir in ground turkey and cook on high for 20 Mins and the let pressure come down on its own. Serve warm.

Nutrition : Calories: 251; Total Fat: 30.9 g; Carbs: 10.1g; Protein: 18.3.

Low Carb Bouillabaisse Fish Stew

Yield: 6 | Total Time: 50 Mins | Prep Time: 10 Mins | Cook Time: 40 Mins

Ingredients

- 1 cup dry white wine
- Juice and zest of 1 orange
- 2 tbsp. olive oil
- 1 large onion, diced
- 2 cloves garlic, minced
- 1 tsp dried basil
- 1/2 tsp dried thyme
- 1/2 tsp salt
- 1/4 tsp ground black pepper
- 4 cups fish stock, chicken stock can also be used
- 1 can diced tomatoes, drained
- 1 bay leaf
- 400g boneless, skinless white fish fillet (ex. cod)
- 400g prawns peeled and deveined
- 400g mussels in their shells
- Juice of 1/2 lemon
- 1/4 cup fresh Italian (flat leaf) parsley

Directions

1. Set your instant pot on manual high and heat oil; add the onion and fry all the vegetables until almost tender; add the garlic, basil, thyme, salt, and pepper. Pour in the wine and bring to a boil. Add the fish stock, orange zest, tomatoes, and bay leaf and stir to combine.

2. Lock lid and cook on high for 1 hour. Quick release the pressure and set on manual high; toss the fish and prawns with the lemon juice and stir into the broth in the pot. Cook for about 20 Mins and then add in the mussels right at the end and allow to steam for 20 Mins with the lid on.

Nutrition : Calories: 310: Fat: 30.7g; Carbs: 4.8g; Protein: 3.7g

Instant Pot Thai Nut Chicken

Yield: 4 | Total Time: 2 Hours 10 Mins | Prep Time: 10 Mins | Cook Time: 2 Hours

Ingredients

- 8 boneless skinless chicken thighs (about 2 pounds)
- ½ cup coconut flour
- 3/4 cup creamy nut butter
- 1/2 cup orange juice
- 1/4 cup diabetic apricot jam
- 2 tablespoons sesame oil
- 2 tablespoons soy sauce
- 2 tablespoons teriyaki sauce
- 2 tablespoons hoisin sauce
- 1 can coconut milk
- 3/4 cup water
- 1 cup chopped roasted almonds or any of the other
- nuts on green list

Directions

1. Place coconut flour in a large resealable plastic bag. Add chicken, a few pieces at a time, and shake to coat. Transfer to a greased instant pot. In a small bowl, combine the nut butter, orange juice, jam, oil, soy sauce, teriyaki sauce, hoisin sauce and 3/4 cup coconut milk; pour over chicken. Lock lid and cook on high for 2 hours. Let pressure come down on its own Sprinkle with nuts before serving.

Nutrition : Calories: 363: Fat: 18.2g; Carbs: 11.6g; Protein: 38.7g

Tasty Instant Pot Greek Fish Stew

Yield: 5 | Total Time: 30 Mins | Prep Time: 10 Mins | Cook Time: 20 Mins

Ingredients

- 5 large white fish fillets
- 1 large red onion, chopped
- 4 cloves of garlic
- 1 leek, sliced
- 1 carrot, chopped
- 3 sticks celery, chopped
- 1 can tomatoes
- 1/2 tsp. saffron threads
- 8 cups fish stock
- 2 tbsp. fresh lemon juice
- 1 tbsp. lemon zest
- handful parsley leaves chopped
- handful mint leaves chopped

Directions

1. Combine all ingredients in your instant pot and lock lid; cook on high for 20 Mins and then release pressure naturally. Serve with gluten-free bread.

Nutrition : Calories: 443; Total Fat: 18.4 g; Carbs: 9.7 g; Dietary Fiber: 1.8 g; Sugars: 3.5 g; Protein: 58.8 g; Cholesterol: 153 mg; Sodium: 871 mg

Pressure Cooker Vegetable and Fish Stew

Yield: 4 | Total Time: 34 Mins | Prep Time: 15 Mins | Cook Time: 19 Mins

Ingredients

- 2 tbsp. extra-virgin olive oil
- 1 red onion, sliced
- 2 jalapeño peppers, seeds removed and diced
- 4 cups sliced green cabbage
- 1 carrot, peeled and chopped
- 4 cups crushed tomatoes
- 2 cup diced white fish filet
- 4 cup vegetable broth
- 3 tbsp. apple cider vinegar
- 2 tsp. Stevia
- ½ tsp. salt
- ¼ tsp. black pepper

Directions

1. Heat extra virgin olive oil in an instant pot set on sauté mode and stir in red onion, jalapenos, cabbage, and carrot; sauté for about 7 Mins or until almost tender.
2. Stir in tomatoes, fish, broth, apple cider vinegar, and Stevia, salt and pepper until well combined. Lock lid and cook on high pressure for 12 Mins. Let pressure come down naturally. Serve hot.

Nutrition : Calories: 222; Total Fat: 19.7 g; Carbs: 13.7 g; Dietary Fiber: 5.9 g; Sugars: 6.3 g; Protein: 18.9 g; Cholesterol: 0 mg; Sodium: 112 mg

Easy Cheesy Turkey Stew

Yield: 5 | Total Time: 30 Mins | Prep Time: 5 Mins | Cook Time: 25 Mins

Ingredients

- 2 tbsp. coconut oil
- 1/2 red onion
- 1 lb. ground turkey
- 2 cups coconut milk
- 2 garlic cloves
- 1 tbsp. mustard
- 2 cups riced cauliflower
- 1 tsp salt
- 1 tsp. black pepper
- 1 tsp. thyme
- 1 tsp. celery salt
- 1 tsp. garlic powder

Directions

1. Melt coconut oil in an instant pot, add garlic and onion and cook until fragrant. Stir in ground turkey until crumbled.
2. Stir in cauliflower and spices until well mixed. Cook until meat is browned. Stir in coconut milk and lock lid. Cook on high for 20 Mins and then let pressure come down on its own. Stir in shredded cheese and serve.

Nutrition : Calories: 475; Total Fat: 39 g; Carbs: 10.5g; Protein: 22.7g

Instant Pot Beef and Sweet Potato Stew

Yield: 6 | Total Time: 35 Mins | Prep Time: 10 Mins | Cook Time: 25 Mins

Ingredients

- 4 tablespoons olive oil
- 2 pounds ground beef
- 3 cups beef stock
- 2 sweet potatoes, peeled and diced
- 1 clove garlic, minced
- 1 onion, diced
- 1 (14-oz) can petite minced tomatoes
- 1 (14-oz) can tomato sauce
- 3-4 tbsp. chili powder
- ¼ tsp. oregano
- 2 tsp. salt
- ½ tsp. black pepper
- Cilantro, optional, for garnish

Directions

1. Brown the beef in a pan over medium heat; drain excess fat and then transfer it to an instant pot. Stir in the remaining ingredients and lock lid; cook on high for 25 Mins and then release pressure naturally. Garnish with cilantro and serve warm.

Nutrition : Calories: 240; Total Fat: 21.6 g; Carbs: 12 g; Dietary Fiber: 3.5 g; Sugars: 4.2 g; Protein: 30.3 g; Cholesterol: 81 mg; Sodium: 1201 mg

Instant Pot Coconut Fish Stew

Yield: 1 Serving | Total Time: 52 Mins | Prep Time: 10 Mins | Cook Time: 42 Mins

Ingredients

- 1 tablespoon olive oil
- 1 red onion
- 1 tablespoon onion powder
- 150g tilapia filet
- ¼ cup coarsely chopped celery
- 2 cloves garlic
- 1 ½ cups vegetable broth
- ½ teaspoon parsley
- ½ teaspoon basil
- White pepper
- Sea salt

Directions

1. Heat oil in your instant pot set over manual high heat; sauté onion until fragrant and then add in the fish. Cook for about 6 Mins per side or until browned. Add in the remaining ingredients and lock lid; cook on high for 30 Mins and then let pressure come down on its own.

Nutrition : Calories: 237; Fat: 18.4g; Carbs: 5.4g; Protein: 23.6g

Instant Pot Loaded Protein Stew

Yields: 2 | Total Time: 1 Hour 5 Mins | Prep Time: 5 Mins | Cook Time: 1 Hour

Ingredients

- 1-pound ground chicken
- 2 minced cloves garlic
- 2 large carrots, grated
- 1 medium red bell pepper, diced
- 1 teaspoon Stevia
- 1/4 cup low-sodium soy sauce
- 1/4 tsp. crushed red pepper flakes
- 1/4 cup ketchup

Directions

1. Combine all ingredients in your instant pot and cook on high setting for 1 hour. Shred the chicken and return to the pot.

Nutritional Information per Serving:

Calories: 262; Total Fat: 8.6 g; Carbs: 11.1g; Dietary Fiber: 1.4 g; Sugars: 7.7 g; Protein: 34.8 g; Cholesterol: 101 mg; Sodium: 1170 mg

Instant Pot Low Carb Mussel Stew

Yield: 4 | Total Time: 1 Hour 40 Mins | Prep Time: 10 Mins | Cook Time: 1 Hour 30 Mins

Ingredients:

- 1kg fresh or frozen, cleaned mussels
- 3 tbsp. olive oil
- 4 cloves garlic, minced
- 1 Large onion, finely diced
- 1 punnet mushrooms, diced
- 2 cans diced tomatoes
- 2 tbsp. oregano
- ½ tbsp. basil
- ½ tsp. black pepper
- 1 tsp. paprika
- dash red chili flakes
- 3/4 cup water

Directions

1. Set your instant pot on manual high and fry in onions, garlic, shallots and mushrooms; stir in the remaining ingredients, except mussels. Lock lid and cook on high for 1 hour; let pressure come down and then set on manual high. Add cleaned mussels to the pot and cook for 30 more Mins
2. Ladle your mussels into bowls with plenty of broth. If any mussels didn't open up during cooking, toss those as well. Enjoy!

Nutrition : Calories: 228; Total Fat: 9.9g; Carbs- 32.1g; Protein: 4.69g

Scrumptious Beef Stew

Yield: 6 | Total Time: 30 Mins | Prep Time: 5 Mins | Cook Time: 25 Mins

Ingredients

- 2 pounds beef stew meat
- 4 tbsp. extra virgin olive oil
- 3 cloves garlic, minced
- 1/4 cup tomato paste
- 4 large carrots, diced
- 2 medium potatoes, diced
- 2/3 cup chopped red onion
- 1 tsp. oregano
- 1 cup beef broth
- 1 ½ cups cooked peas

Directions

1. Heat oil u sauté mode in your instant pot; stir in meat and garlic and cook until browned. Add tomato paste, carrots, potato, onion, oregano and broth and lock lid. Cook on manual for 20 Mins and then release pressure naturally. Stir in cooked peas to serve.

Nutrition : Calories: 422; Total Fat: 22.3 g; Carbs: 25.2 g; Dietary Fiber: 5.6 g; Sugars: 7.3 g; Protein: 51 g; Cholesterol: 135 mg; Sodium: 277 mg

Turkish Split Pea Stew

Yield: 4 | Total Time: 25 Mins | Prep Time: 10 Mins | Cook Time: 15 Mins

Ingredients

- 1 red onion, chopped
- 1½ tablespoons olive oil
- 4-5 cloves garlic, chopped
- ½ cup chopped tomatoes
- 2 cups split peas, rinsed
- 1 celery stick, chopped
- 1 medium carrot, chopped
- 1½ teaspoons cumin powder
- 1 teaspoon paprika powder
- ¼ teaspoon chili powder
- ¼ teaspoon cinnamon
- 6 cups vegetable stock
- 2 tablespoons lemon juice
- 1 bay leaf
- ½ teaspoon sea salt
- Chopped scallions and chives for garnish

Directions

1. Turn your instant pot on sauté mode and heat oil; add onion, celery and carrots and sauté for 4 Mins. Stir in the remaining ingredients and press the cancel or warm button. Lock lid and press manual high for 10 Mins. When done, let pressure release naturally and then serve topped with chopped scallions or chives and lemon wedge.

Nutrition : Calories: 205; Total Fat: 19.7 g; Carbs: 15.9 g; Dietary Fiber: 6.8 g; Sugars: 7.3 g; Protein: 5.9 g; Cholesterol: 0 mg; Sodium: 465 mg

Delicious Seafood Stew

Yield: 6 | Total Time: 35 Mins | Prep Time: 15 Mins | Cook Time: 20 Mins

Ingredients:

- 3 tablespoons olive oil
- 2 pounds seafood (1 pound large shrimp & 1 pound scallops)
- 1/2 cup chopped white onion
- 3 garlic cloves, minced
- 1 tbsp. tomato paste
- 1 can (28 oz.) crushed tomatoes
- 4 cups vegetable broth
- 1 pound yellow potatoes, diced
- 1 tsp. dried basil
- 1 tsp. dried thyme
- 1 tsp. dried oregano
- 1/8 tsp. cayenne pepper
- 1/4 tsp. crush red pepper flakes
- 1/2 tsp. celery salt
- salt and pepper
- handful of chopped parsley

Directions:

1. Mix all ingredients, except seafood, in your instant pot and lock lid; cook on high for about 15 Mins. Quick release the pressure and then stir in seafood and continue; lock lid and cook on high for five Mins and then let pressure come down on its own. Serve hot with crusty gluten-free bread and garnished with parsley.

Nutrition : Calories: 323; Total Fat: 15.3 g; Carbs: 7.7 g; Dietary Fiber: 0.8 g; Sugars: 1.9 g; Protein: 57.1 g; Cholesterol: 478 mg; Sodium: 1323 mg

Curried Chicken Stew

Yield: 2 | Total Time: 2 Hours | Prep Time: 20 Mins | Cook Time: 1 Hour 40 Mins

Ingredients:

- 2 bone-in chicken thighs
- 2 tbsp. olive oil
- 3 carrots, diced
- 1 sweet onion, chopped
- 1 cup coconut milk
- 1/4 cup hot curry paste
- Toasted almonds
- Coriander
- Sour cream to serve

Directions

1. Set your instant pot to manual high setting; heat oil and cook chicken for 8 Mins or until browned. Stir in carrots and onion and cook for about 3 Mins.
2. In a bowl, combine curry paste and coconut milk; whisk until well blended and pour over chicken mixture.
3. Lock lid and cook on high for 1 ½ hours and then let pressure come down naturally.
   Serve the stew topped with toasted almonds, coriander, fresh chili and a dollop of sour cream.

Nutrition : Calories: 409; Total Fat: 15.5 g; Carbs: 10.7 g; Dietary Fiber: 1.9 g; Sugars: 3.4 g; Protein: 55.3 g; Cholesterol: 231 mg; Sodium: 609 mg

Beef Chuck & Green Cabbage Stew

Yield: 2 | Total Time: 9 Hours 20 Mins | Prep Time: 20 Mins | Cook Time: 3 Hours

Ingredients

- 1 packet frozen baby carrots
- 2 onions, roughly chopped
- 1 cup chopped cabbage
- 4 garlic cloves, smashed
- 2 bay leaves
- 4 pieces of beef chuck with marrow
- Salt & pepper
- 1 thin diced tomato, drained
- 1 cup chicken stock

Directions

1. Place the baby carrots and chopped onions into the bottom of your instant pot. Layer the cabbage wedges on top and add the crushed garlic cloves and bay leaves.
2. Season the beef shanks generously with salt and pepper then add them on top of the veggies.
3. Pour in the diced tomatoes and broth before putting on the lid. Set the pot on high for 3 hours. Let pressure come down naturally.
4. Once ready, allow to cool then pack in freezer friendly bags or jars and freeze until when you are ready to eat.

Nutrition : Calories: 394; Total Fat: 11.4 g; Carbs: 13.1 g; Dietary Fiber: 4.1 g; Sugars: 6.8 g; Protein: 54.6 g; Cholesterol: 152 mg; Sodium: 509 mg

Madras Lamb Stew

Yield: 2 | Total Time: 2 Hours 25 Mins | Prep Time: 25 Mins | Cook Time: 2 Hours

Ingredients:

- 3 fatty lamb chops
- 3 tbsp. coconut milk
- 2 cups water
- 3 tbsp. Red Curry Paste
- 2 tbsp. Thai fish sauce
- 1 tbsp. dried onion flakes
- 2 tbsp. fresh red chilies, minced
- 1 tbsp. sugar
- 1 tbsp. ground cumin
- 1 tbsp. ground coriander
- 1/8 tsp. ground cloves
- 1/8 tsp. ground nutmeg
- 1 tbsp. ground ginger

Toppings when ready to serve:

- 2 tbsp. coconut milk powder
- 1 tbsp. red curry paste
- 2 tbsp. sugar
- 1/4 cup cashews, roughly chopped
- 1/4 cup fresh cilantro, chopped

Directions

1. Place the raw lamb chops in an instant pot; add the coconut milk, water, red curry paste, fish sauce, onion flakes, chilies, cumin, coriander, cloves, nutmeg, and ginger.
2. Cover and cook on high for 2 hours.
3. Let the lamb curry cool completely then pack in freezer friendly bags or jars.
4. After thawing and heating, just before serving, whisk the coconut milk powder, curry paste and sweetener into the sauce
5. Break the meat into pieces and stir into the sauce together with the chopped cashews.
6. Garnish with fresh coriander.

Nutrition : Calories: 484; Total Fat: 19.4 g; Carbs: 10.7 g; Dietary Fiber: 1.8 g; Sugars: 4.5 g; Protein: 48.8 g; Cholesterol: 223 mg; Sodium: 987 mg

Curried Goat Stew

Yield: 4 | Total Time: 1 Hour 5 Mins | Prep Time: 5 Mins | Cook Time: 1 Hour

Ingredients

- 4 goat chops
- 2 tbsp. olive oil
- 3 carrots, cut in 2-inch pieces
- 1 sweet onion, cut in thin wedges
- 1/2 cup unsweetened coconut milk
- 1/4 cup mild curry paste
- Toasted almond
- Coriander
- Fresh green or red chili

Directions

1. Combine all ingredients in an instant pot and lock lid. Cook on high for 1 hour and let pressure come down on its own.
2. Serve topped with toasted almonds and a dollop yogurt.

Nutrition : Calories: 423; Total Fat: 17.2 g; Carbs: 8.8 g; Dietary Fiber: 4.9 g; Sugars: 2.3 g; Protein: 31.2 g; Cholesterol: 128 mg; Sodium: 1012 mg

Instant Pot Lemon Chicken Stew

Yield: 2 | Total Time: 1 Hour 40 Mins | Prep Time: 10 Mins | Cook Time: 1 Hour 30 Mins

Ingredients:

- 2 carrots, chopped
- 2 ribs celery, chopped
- 1 onion, chopped
- 10 large green olives
- 4 cloves garlic, crushed
- 2 bay leaves
- ½ tsp. dried oregano
- ¼ tsp. salt
- ¼ tsp. pepper
- 6 boneless skinless chicken thighs
- ¾ cup chicken stock
- ¼ cup almond flour
- 2 tbsp. lemon juice
- ½ cup chopped fresh parsley
- grated zest of 1 lemon

Directions

1. In your instant pot, combine carrots, celery, onion, olives, garlic, bay leaves, oregano, salt and pepper. Arrange chicken pieces on top of vegetables. Add broth and ¾ cup water. Lock lid and cook on high setting for 1 ½ hours. Let pressure come down naturally. Discard bay leaves.
2. In a small bowl, whisk together a cup of cooking liquid and flour until very smooth; whisk in lemon juice and pour the mixture into your pot. Cook on manual high for about 15 Mins or until thickened.
3. In a small bowl, mix together lemon zest and chopped parsley; sprinkled over the chicken mixture and serve. Enjoy!

Nutrition : Calories: 392; Total Fat: 19.4 g; Carbs: 11.2 g; Dietary Fiber: 6.7 g; Sugars: 2.4 g; Protein: 31.2 g; Cholesterol: 103 mg; Sodium: 1213 mg

Hearty Lamb & Cabbage Stew

Yield: 4 | Total Time: 2 Hours 45 Mins | Prep Time: 15 Mins | Cook Time: 2 hours 30 Mins

Ingredients

- 2 tbsp. coconut oil
- 200g lamb chops, bone in
- 1 lamb or beef stock cube
- 2 cups water
- 1 cup shredded cabbage
- 1 onion, sliced
- 2 carrots, chopped
- 2 sticks celery, chopped
- 1 tsp. dried thyme
- 1 tbsp. balsamic vinegar
- 1 tbsp. almond flour

Directions

1. Set your instant pot to manual high and heat in oil; brown in the lamb chops and then add in the remaining ingredients. Cook on high for 2 hours and then let pressure come down naturally. Remove bones from the meat.
2. To thicken your sauce, ladle ¼ cup of sauce into a bowl and whisk in almond flour. Return to the pot and stir well; lock lid and cook for 30 Mins on manual high.

Nutrition : Calories: 384; Total Fat: 19.4 g; Carbs: 6.8 g; Dietary Fiber: 4.8 g; Sugars: 1.5 g; Protein: 38.4 g; Cholesterol: 223 mg; Sodium: 822 mg

Rosemary-Garlic Beef Stew

Yield: 2 | Total Time: 2 Hours 15 Mins | Prep Time: 15 Mins | Cook Time: 2 Hours

Ingredients:

- 3 medium carrots
- 3 sticks celery
- 1 medium onion
- 2 tbsp. olive oil
- 4 cloves garlic, minced
- 200g beef chuck
- Salt and pepper
- ¼ cup almond flour
- 2 cups beef stock
- 2 tbsp. Dijon mustard
- 1 tbsp. Worcestershire sauce
- 1 tbsp. soy sauce
- 1 tbsp. xylitol
- ½ tbsp. dried rosemary
- ½ tsp. thyme

Directions

1. Combine all ingredients in an instant pot and cook on high setting for 2 hours. Let pressure come down naturally.

Nutritional Information per Serving:

Calories: 419; Total Fat: 21.6 g; Carbs: 13.9 g; Dietary Fiber: 4.6 g; Sugars: 8.4 g; Protein: 39.6 g; Cholesterol: 89 mg; Sodium: 1626 mg

Instant Pot Oxtail Stew

Yield: 2 | Total Time: 2 Hours 10 Mins | Prep Time: 10 Mins | Cook Time: 2 Hours

Ingredients

- ½ pound oxtail
- 1 cup grated cabbage
- 1/2 cup grated carrots
- 2 large red onions, chopped
- 1 large bunch celery, chopped
- 1/2 cup diced tomatoes
- 2 jelly stock cubes
- 4 cups water
- 1 tbsp. crushed garlic
- 1 branch rosemary
- 2 bay leaves
- Grated cheese to serve

Directions

1. Place all ingredients except cheese into an instant pot and cook on high setting for 2 hours. Let pressure come down naturally. Serve sprinkled with grated cheese.

Nutritional Information per Serving:

Calories: 414; Total Fat: 14.3 g; Carbs: 9.1 g; Dietary Fiber: 7.6g; Sugars: 1.4 g; Protein: 20.2 g; Cholesterol: 96 mg; Sodium: 812 mg

Pressure Cooked Lamb-Bacon Stew

Yield: 2 | Total Time: 2 Hours 20 Mins | Prep Time: 20 Mins | Cook Time: 2 Hours

Ingredients

- 2 cloves garlic, minced
- 1 leek, sliced
- 2 celery ribs, diced
- 1 cup sliced button mushrooms
- 2 Vidalia onions, thinly sliced
- 2 tbsp. butter
- 2 cups chicken stock
- 200g lamb, cut in cubes
- 4 oz. cream cheese
- 1 cup heavy cream
- 1 packet bacon – cooked crisp, and crumbled
- 1 tsp. salt
- 1 tsp. pepper
- 1 tsp. garlic powder
- 1 tsp. thyme

Directions

1. Set your instant pot on manual high setting and melt in butter; sear lamb meat until browned. Add in garlic, leeks, celery, mushrooms, onions, and cook for about 5 Mins; stir in the remaining ingredients and lock lid. Cook on high for 2 hours and then let pressure come down on its own.

Nutrition : Calories: 365; Total Fat: 19.2 g; Carbs: 12.9 g; Dietary Fiber: 6.6 g; Sugars: 4.3 g; Protein: 21.1 g; Cholesterol: 91 mg; Sodium: 843 mg

Instant Pot Low Carb Vegetable Stew

Yield: 1 Serving | Total Time: 15 Mins | Prep Time: 5 Mins | Cook Time: 10 Mins

Ingredients

- 1 medium cauliflower
- 8 cups water
- 1 tsp. lemon juice
- 3 tsp. ground flax seeds
- 3 cups spinach
- 1 tsp. cayenne pepper
- 1 tsp. black pepper
- 1 tsp. soy sauce

Directions:

1. Core cauliflower and cut the florets into large pieces; reserve stems for juicing.
2. Add cauliflower to an instant pot and add water; lock lid and cook on high pressure for 10 Mins. Release pressure naturally and then transfer the cauliflower. Stir in the remaining ingredients and serve hot or warm.

Nutrition : Calories: 198; Total Fat: 11.2 g; Carbs: 11.1 g; Dietary Fiber: 6.3 g; Sugars: 2.9 g; Protein: 1.8 g; Cholesterol: 0 mg; Sodium: 213 mg

Best Beef Stew for a King!

Yield: 2 | Total Time: 2 Hours 25 Mins | Prep Time: 15 Mins | Cook Time: 2 Hours 10 Mins

Ingredients

- 200g beef meat, cubed
- 1 tsp. Salt
- 1 tsp. pepper
- 1 medium onion, finely chopped
- 2 celery ribs, sliced
- 2 cloves of garlic, minced
- 1 can tomato paste
- 3 cups beef stock
- 2 tbsp. Worcestershire sauce
- 1 cup frozen mixed veggies
- 1 tablespoon almond flour
- 1 tablespoon water

Directions

1. Combine all ingredients except flour, frozen veggies, and water in your instant pot.
2. Cook on high setting for 2 hours. Let pressure come down on its own.
3. Stir together water and flour; stir into the pot and then add in veggies; lock lid and cook for 10 Mins.

Nutrition : Calories: 368; Total Fat: 14.3 g; Carbs: 13.6 g; Dietary Fiber: 5.8 g; Sugars: 6.9 g; Protein: 44.6 g; Cholesterol: 89 mg; Sodium: 2691 mg

INSTANT POT KETO BEEF RECIPES

Healthy Italian Beef & Cabbage Stir-Fry

Yield: 4 | Total Time: 30 Mins | Prep Time: 10 Mins | Cook Time: 20 Mins

Ingredients

- 2 pounds ground beef
- 4 tablespoons butter
- 4 cups green cabbage, shredded
- 2 garlic cloves, finely chopped
- ½ cup leeks, thinly sliced
- 1 tsp onion powder
- ½ cup fresh basil
- 1 tbsp. tomato paste
- 1 tbsp. white wine vinegar
- 1 tsp salt
- ¼ tsp pepper
- 1 cup sour cream
- 4 cups green salad to serve

Directions

1. Heat half the butter in an instant pot and sauté the cabbage for about 10 Mins or until tender; stir in onion powder, vinegar, salt and pepper and cook for 3 Mins. Transfer the sautéed cabbage to a bowl and set aside.
2. Heat the remaining butter in the pot and sauté leeks and garlic for 1 minute or until fragrant; stir in meat and fry for about 5 Mins. Stir in tomato paste and lock lid. Cook on high for 5 Mins and then let pressure come down on its own. Stir in basil and sautéed cabbage cook on manual high for 2 Mins and then remove from heat. Serve drizzled with sour cream and green salad on the side.

Nutrition : Calories: 296; Total Fat: 14.3 g; Carbs: 8.3 g; Dietary Fiber: 1.6 g; Sugars: 4.2 g; Protein: 32.76 g; Cholesterol: 62 mg; Sodium: 157 mg

Instant Pot Beef Shred Rolls serve with Chilled Lemon Juice

Yield: 3 | Total Time: 30 Mins | Prep Time: 10 Mins | Cook Time: 20 Mins

Ingredients

- 300g beef steak
- 1 yellow pepper, sliced thin lengthwise
- 1 white onion, sliced lengthwise
- 6 pcs. butter lettuce
- 2 tsp. mayo
- 1/8 tsp. chili flakes
- 3 glasses freshly squeezed chilled lemon juice to serve

Directions

1. Place the butter lettuce on a serving plate.
2. Set your instant pot on manual high and heat oil; fry beef for 5 Mins per side. Add broth and lock lid; cook on high for 10 Mins and then remove beef. Shred thinly. Spread mayo on the lettuce and top with the shredded beef.
3. Place pepper slices and onions on top and season with chili flakes. Fold to form the rolls, securing with toothpicks. Serve with fresh lemon juice.

Nutrition : Calories: 338; Total Fat: 25 g; Carbs: 2.4 g; Dietary Fiber: 1.7 g; Sugars: 0.3 g; Protein: 24 g; Cholesterol: 214 mg; Sodium: 1209 mg

Delicious Instant Pot Steak with Parsley & Arugula

Yield: 3 | Total Time: 25 Mins | Prep Time: 10 Mins | Cook Time: 15 Mins

Ingredients

- 2 (10-ounce) boneless steaks
- 2 tbsp. extra virgin olive oil, and extra for drizzling
- 2 tbsp. fresh lemon juice
- 2 ounces shaved Parmesan
- 4 ounces caper berries, halved if large
- 1 red chili, thinly sliced
- ¼ medium red onion, thinly sliced
- 1 bunch arugula, tough stems removed
- Kosher salt and pepper
- 1 cup parsley

Directions

1. Heat oil in an instant pot set on manual high; sprinkle steaks with salt and pepper and add to the pot. Cook for about 5 Mins per side or until browned. Lock lid and cook for 3 Mins on high. Let pressure come down naturally.
2. In a medium bowl, toss together caper berries, chili, onion, arugula, parsley and Parmesan cheese; drizzle with lemon juice and toss to coat well. Season to taste.
3. Drizzle the grilled steaks with extra virgin olive oil and season with more salt and pepper. Serve the steaks with the salad.

Nutrition : Calories: 376; Fat: 24.3g; Carbs: 7.8g; Protein: 21.3g

Filet Mignon with Caramelized Onions

Yield: 3 | Total Time: 1 Hour | Prep Time: 45 Mins | Cook Time: 15 Mins

Ingredients

- 3 filet mignon steaks
- ¼ cup olive oil
- 1 tbsp. Dijon mustard
- ¼ cup aged balsamic vinegar
- 2 cups medium sliced onions
- 100g goat cheese or your favourite cheese, crumbled
- 1 tbsp. butter
- 1 tsp. sugar
- 2 tsp. dried rosemary
- Cracked black pepper
- Seasoned salt

Directions

1. Generously season the steaks with the cracked black pepper and seasoned salt then place them in a dish in a single layer.
2. In a medium bowl, combine the vinegar, olive oil, rosemary and mustard until well incorporated. Pour this over the filets and coat both sides. Cover the dish with cling wrap and transfer to your fridge to marinate for 30 Mins.
3. Meanwhile, melt the butter in an instant pot set on manual high and cook the onion slices for 5 Mins until the onions become caramelized.
4. Add in the steak and cook for about 5 Mins per side or until golden browned.
5. Top with cheese and lock lid for 2 Mins. Let pressure come down naturally and then serve the cheesy steak hot. Enjoy!

Nutrition : Calories: 411; Fat: 39.1g; Carbs: 9.2g; Protein: 20.1g

Healthy Beef Chili served with Avocado and Green Onions

Yields: 6 | Total Time: 45 Mins | Prep Time: 10 Mins | Cook Time: 35 Mins

Ingredients

- 2 lb. ground beef
- 3 slices bacon, cut into thin strips
- ¼ yellow onion, chopped
- 2 cloves garlic, minced
- 1 green bell pepper, chopped
- 2 celery stalks, chopped
- 1/2 cup sliced baby Bellas
- 2 tbsp. smoked paprika
- 2 tsp. dried oregano
- 2 tsp. ground cumin
- 2 tbsp. chili powder
- 2 cup low-sodium beef broth
- 2 avocados, sliced avocado
- 2 cups sliced green onions
- 1 cup shredded cheddar
- 1 cup sour cream
- A pinch of salt
- A pinch of pepper

Directions

1. Cook bacon in an instant pot on manual high setting until crispy; remove bacon from the pot and add in onion, mushrooms, celery and pepper. Cook for about 6 Mins and then stir in garlic for about 1 minute. Push the veggies on the side and add in beef. Cook until it is no longer pink. Stir in paprika, oregano, cumin, chili powder, salt and pepper. Cook for about 2 Mins and then stir in broth; lock lid and cook on high setting for 20 Mins. Let pressure come down on its own.
2. Ladle the chili into serving bowls and top each serving with reserved bacon, cheese, sour cream avocado and green onions.

Nutrition : Calories: 413; Fat: 31.9g; Carbs: 14.3g; Protein: 21.7g

Ground Beef with Veggies

Yields: 4 | Total Time: 30 Mins | Prep Time: 5 Mins | Cook Time: 25 Mins

Ingredients

- 1 lb. lean ground beef
- 2 medium (6 to 8 inches each) zucchinis, diced
- 1 tbsp. coconut oil
- 1-2 cloves garlic, minced
- 2 medium tomatoes, diced
- 2 tbsp. dried oregano
- 1/2 yellow onion, diced

Directions

1. Rinse and prepare the veggies.
2. Set your instant pot on manual high and melt coconut oil; stir in onions and sauté for about 4 Mins or until translucent.
3. Roll ground beef into small balls and add to the pot along with oregano and garlic; cook for about 5 Mins. Add tomatoes and zucchini and lock lid. Cook on high for 20 Mins and then let pressure come down on its own.
4. Serve and enjoy!

Nutrition : Calories: 287; Total Fat: 26.9g; Carbs: 6.1g; Protein: 12.3g

Herbed London Broil with Lemon Garlic Butter Zucchini Noodles

Yield: 4 | Total Time: 40 Mins | Prep Time: 10 Mins | Cook Time: 30 Mins

Ingredients

- 2 pounds lean London broil, sliced thinly into strips
- 2 clove garlic, minced
- 2 red onion, minced
- 1 cup beef broth or water

- Chopped Italian parsley
- Pinch of rosemary
- 1 teaspoon thyme
- Pinch of salt & pepper

Lemon Garlic Butter Zucchini Noodles

- 3 tablespoons butter
- 4 cloves garlic, minced
- ½ teaspoon red chili pepper flakes
- 4 medium zucchinis, spiralized

- 1 tablespoon hot sauce
- 1 cup chopped cilantro
- Juice of 1/2 lemon

Directions:

1. **Prepare the Zucchini noodles:** Melt butter in a large skillet; stir in garlic for 2 Mins or until fragrant. Stir in red pepper flakes, hot sauce and lemon juice. Cook for 1 minute and then stir in zucchini and cook for about 3 Mins until well coated with butter sauce. Season with salt and pepper and remove from heat.
2. Coat beef with salt and pepper and add to an instant pot along with beef broth and
3. herbs; lock lid and cook on high for 30 Mins. Naturally release the pressure and then serve beef with zucchini noodles garnished with parsley.

Nutrition : Calories: 201; Total Fat: 6.6 g; Carbs: 1.4 g; Dietary Fiber: 0.4 g; Sugars: 0.6 g; Protein: 31.7 g; Cholesterol: 89 mg; Sodium: 257 mg

Low Carb Beef & Sweet Potato Dish

Yield: 6 | Total Time: 35 Mins | Prep Time: 10 Mins | Cook Time: 25 Mins

Ingredients

- 4 tablespoons olive oil
- 2 pounds ground beef
- 3 cups beef stock
- 2 sweet potatoes, peeled and diced
- 1 clove garlic, minced
- 1 onion, diced
- 1 (14-oz) can petite minced tomatoes
- 1 (14-oz) can tomato sauce
- 3-4 tbsp. chili powder
- ¼ tsp. oregano
- 2 tsp. salt
- ½ tsp. black pepper
- Cilantro, optional, for garnish

Directions

1. Brown the beef in a pan over medium heat; drain excess fat and then transfer it to an instant pot. Stir in the remaining ingredients and lock lid; cook on high for 25 Mins and then release pressure naturally. Garnish with cilantro and serve warm.

Nutrition : Calories: 240; Total Fat: 21.6 g; Carbs: 12 g; Dietary Fiber: 3.5 g; Sugars: 4.2 g; Protein: 30.3 g; Cholesterol: 81 mg; Sodium: 1201 mg

Asparagus & Steak Bowl

Yield: 4 | Total Time: 25 Mins | Prep Time: 10 | Cook Time: 15 Mins

Ingredients

- Olive oil cooking spray
- ¾ pound beef top sirloin steak, diced
- 1/2 tsp. low-sodium steak seasoning
- 1/2 cup chopped red bell pepper
- 1/2 cup chopped red onion
- 1 cup frozen asparagus cuts
- 2 ½ tbsp. soy sauce
- 1 avocado, sliced

Directions

1. Coat an instant pot with cooking spray and set on manual high; sprinkle beef with the steak seasoning and cook in the pot for about 3 Mins; add bell pepper and red onion and cook for 3 Mins more or until beef is browned. Add asparagus and lock lid. Cook on high for 5 Mins and then let the pressure come down on its own.
2. Stir soy sauce in the beef mixture and serve with avocado.

Nutrition : Calories: 325; Total Fat: 38.2g; Carbs: 10.4 g; Protein: 26g

Crunchy Steak Salad

Yield: 2 | Total Time: 15 Mins | Prep Time: 10 Mins | Cook Time: 5 Mins

Ingredients

- 250g steak
- 1/4 cup tamari soy sauce
- 1 tablespoon avocado oil
- 1 tablespoon olive oil
- 1/2 tablespoon lemon juice
- 4 radishes, sliced
- 6 cherry tomatoes, halved
- 1/2 red bell pepper, sliced
- 2 cups salad greens
- ¼ teaspoon salt

Directions

1. Pour tamari sauce in a large bowl; add in steak and toss to coat well; cover and let marinate for a few hours before cooking.
2. In another bowl, combine green salad, radishes, tomatoes, bell peppers, lemon juice, olive oil and salt; toss to coat well and set aside.
3. Heat avocado oil in an instant pot on manual high setting; cook the steak for about 8 Mins per side or until cooked through and browned on the outside. Lock lid and cook for 4 Mins and then quick release pressure and then slice.
4. Divide the salad between two plates and top each with steak slices.

Nutrition : Calories: 500; Total Fat: 37 g; Carbs: 4g; Protein: 18g

Mango Chili Beef Stir Fry

Yield: 4 | Total Time: 30 Mins | Prep Time: 15 Mins | Cook Time: 5 Mins

Ingredients

- ½ tablespoon sesame oil
- 1 tablespoon low-sodium soy sauce
- 1 tablespoon cornstarch
- 1 pound beef steak, diced
- ½ tablespoon peanut oil
- 1 tablespoon minced fresh ginger
- 1 red onion, chopped
- 2 cups snow peas
- 1 tablespoon chili garlic sauce
- 1 mango, peeled, chopped
- 1/8 teaspoon sea salt
- 1/8 teaspoon black pepper
- 2 cups brown rice
- 4 cups water
- Salt

Directions

1. In a mixing bowl, combine sesame oil, soy sauce, cornstarch and chicken; let sit for at least 20 Mins.
2. Set your instant pot on manual high and heat peanut oil and then sauté ginger and onion for about 2 Mins; add snow peas and stir fry for about 1 minute. Add beef with the marinade and stir fry for about 2 Mins or until chicken is browned. Add chili sauce, mango and pepper and lock lid. Cook for 5 Mins on high and then quick release the pressure.

Nutrition : Calories: 377; Total Fat: 28.4g; Carbs: 8.6 g; Protein: 17.9g

Creamy Beef, Red Pepper & Cucumber Salad

Yield: 4 | Total Time: 34 Mins | Prep Time: 5 Mins | Cook Time: 29 Mins

Ingredients

- 400g beef steak
- 1 red onion, sliced
- 3 cucumbers, sliced
- 2 tablespoons fresh chopped chives
- 2 tablespoons mayonnaise
- 1/2 cup sour cream
- Salt & black pepper

Directions

1. Rub beef steak with olive oil, salt and pepper; add to an instant pot and fry on manual high for 7 Mins per side. Transfer to a plate. Add water to the pot and insert a trivet. Place the beef on the trivet and lock lid. Cook on high for 15 Mins and then let pressure come down on its own.
2. Remove beef and shred.
3. In a bowl, combine shred beef, red onion and cucumber.
4. In a small bowl, whisk together mayonnaise, sour cream, chives and pepper until well blended; stir into the cucumber salad until well coated; sprinkle with salt and serve.

Nutrition : Calories: 140; Total Fat: 19.1g; Carbs: 5.5g; Protein: 12.5g

Instant Pot Lemon Beef Steak

Yield: 4 | Total Time: 1 Hour 10 Mins | Prep Time: 10 Mins | Cook Time: 1 Hour

Ingredients

- 2 pounds beef steak
- 1 red onion, minced
- Juice of ½ lemon
- Pinch of lemon zest
- Pinch of saffron
- Pinch of ground coriander
- Pinch of ginger
- Pinch of salt & pepper

Directions:

1. Soak saffron in fresh lemon juice; crush into paste and then add dry spices.
2. Dip beef steak in mixture and rub remaining spices into steak; sprinkle with salt and pepper and wrap in foil. Add water to an instant pot and insert a trivet; place the beef over the trivet and lock lid and cook on manual high for 1 hour.

Nutrition : Calories: 122; Total Fat: 2.6 g; Carbs: 1.9 g; Dietary Fiber: 0.5 g; Sugars: 0.6 g; Protein: 21.4 g; Cholesterol: 64 mg; Sodium: 52 mg

Instant Pot Beef Curry

Yield: 3 | Total Time: 40 Mins | Prep Time: 10 Mins | Cook Time: 30 Mins

Ingredients

- 4 tbsp. coconut oil
- 300 grams beef steak, diced
- ¼ cup beef broth
- Pinch of turmeric
- Dash of onion powder
- 1 tablespoon minced red onion
- Pinch of garlic powder
- ¼ teaspoon curry powder
- Pinch of sea salt
- Pinch of pepper
- Stevia
- Pinch of cayenne

Directions

1. Set your instant pot to manual high, melt in coconut oil and then stir in garlic and onion. Cook until fragrant and stir in beef. In a small bowl, stir together spices, Stevia, and beef broth until dissolved; stir into the beef and lock lid. Cook for 30 Mins and then naturally release the pressure. Serve hot.

Nutrition : Calories: 170; Total Fat: 23.5 g; Carbs: 5.3 g; Dietary Fiber: 0.6 g; Sugars: 0.8 g; Protein: 30.5 g; Cholesterol: 77 mg; Sodium: 255 mg

Steak Salad with Spiced Avocado Dressing

Yield: 2 | Total Time: 39 Mins | Prep Time: 10 Mins | Cook Time: 29 Mins

Ingredients

Salad:
- ¾ pound grilled ribeye, sliced
- 1 cup salad greens
- 1/2 cup sliced cucumber

- ½ cup sliced black olives
- 1 avocado
- 1/2 cup grape tomatoes, halved

Dressing:
- 1 avocado
- 2 tablespoons avocado oil
- 2 tablespoons balsamic vinegar
- 2 tablespoons lime juice

- 1/4 teaspoon red pepper flakes
- 1 cup fresh cilantro
- 1 clove garlic minced
- 1/2 teaspoon sea salt

Directions

1. Rub beef steak with olive oil, salt and pepper; add to an instant pot and fry on manual high for 7 Mins per side. Transfer to a plate. Add water to the pot and insert a trivet. Place the beef on the trivet and lock lid. Cook on high for 15 Mins and then let pressure come down on its own.
2. Remove beef and shred.
3. In a bowl, mix all salad ingredients and set aside.
4. In a blender, blend together all dressing ingredients until very smooth; pour over the salad and toss to coat well. Divide between serving bowls and enjoy!

Nutrition : Calories: 644; Total Fat: 53g; Carbs: 8g; Protein: 27g

Healthy Zucchini Beef Sauté with Avocado

Yield: 2 | Total Time: 25 Mins | Prep Time: 5 Mins | Cook Time: 20 Mins

Ingredients

- 300g beef, sliced into thin strips
- 1 zucchini, sliced into thin strips
- 1/4 cup cilantro, chopped
- 3 cloves of garlic, diced or minced
- 2 tablespoons gluten-free tamari sauce
- 2 tablespoons avocado oil
- 1 avocado, diced

Directions

1. Heat oil in an instant pot set on manual high setting; add in beef and sauté for about 10 Mins or until browned. Stir in zucchini and cook for 5 Mins more or until zucchini is tender. Stir in garlic, cilantro and tamari sauce and lock lid. Cook on high for 5 Mins and then serve right away topped with avocado.

Nutrition : Calories: 300; Total Fat: 40g; Carbs: 5g; Dietary Fiber: 1g; Sugars: 2g; Protein: 31g

Low Carb Ground Beef Tacos with Salsa

Yield: 4 | Total Time: 35 Mins | Prep Time: 10 Mins | Cook Time: 25 Mins

Ingredients

- 500 grams lean ground beef
- 2 clove garlic, minced
- 2 red onions, minced
- 8 lettuce leaves
- A pinch of cayenne pepper
- Fresh chopped cilantro
- Pinch of dried oregano
- Dash of onion powder
- Dash of garlic powder
- Pinch of salt & pepper

Directions:

1. Fry beef in olive oil in an instant pot set on manual high setting until browned; add garlic, onion and spices, and water; lock lid and cook on high for 10 Mins and then release the pressure naturally. Season with salt and serve taco style in romaine lettuce or butter lettuce or with a side of salsa.

Nutrition : Calories: 194; Total Fat: 6.3 g; Carbs: 1.9 g; Dietary Fiber: 0.5 g; Sugars: 0.7 g; Protein: 30.6 g; Cholesterol: 89 mg; Sodium: 67 mg

Pepper Crusted Steak with Garlic Creamed Sautéed Spinach

Yield: 2 | Total Time: 25 Mins | Prep Time: 10 Mins | Cook Time: 15 Mins

Ingredients

- 300 grams lean steak
- 1 tablespoon olive oil
- Dash of Worcestershire sauce

Garlic Creamed Sautéed Spinach

- 2 tablespoons melted butter
- 4 cloves garlic, thinly sliced
- 2 cups fresh spinach, rinsed

- Pinch of salt & pepper
- ½ cup beef broth
- 1 cup of green salad for serving.

- ¼ cup coconut cream
- 1 teaspoon lemon juice
- Sea salt & pepper

Directions

1. Prepare spinach: Melt butter in a skillet and sauté garlic until fragrant. Stir in spinach, lemon juice and coconut cream and cook for about 3 Mins. Stir in salt and pepper and remove from heat.
2. Pound meat until tender and flat; rub with salt and pepper. Heat olive oil in an instant pot set on manual high setting; add meat and cook for about 3 Mins per side. Stir in broth and lock lid; cook on high for 10 Mins and then let pressure come down on its own. Serve over a bowl of creamed spinach topped with Worcestershire sauce and garnished with caramelized onions. Enjoy!

Nutrition : Calories: 189; Total Fat: 6.2 g; Carbs: 0.2 g; Dietary Fiber: 0 g; Sugars: 0.1 g; Protein: 30.4 g; Cholesterol: 89 mg; Sodium: 228 mg

Steak Frites with Rocket & Peppercorn Sauce

Yield: 4 | Total Time: 30 Mins | Prep Time: 15 Mins | Cook Time: 15 Mins

Ingredients

- 4 x 200g beef eye-fillet steaks
- 2 tbsp. extra virgin olive oil
- 1/4 cup red wine
- 55g can green peppercorns, rinsed, drained

- 1/2 cup beef stock
- 1/2 cup crème fraiche
- Handfuls of rocket and chopped parsley

Directions

1. Combine wine and peppercorns in a large bowl; let stand for about 5 Mins.
2. Season steaks with sea salt and black pepper.
3. Heat oil in an instant pot set on manual high and add the steaks; cook for about 3 Mins per side or until cooked to your desired doneness. Add in the wine mixture and stir in crème fraiche and stock; lock lid. Cook on high for 15 Mins and then let pressure come down on its own. Season and serve with rocket and parsley.

Nutrition : Calories: 387; Total Fat: 36 g; Carbs: 5g; Protein: 27g

Lean Steak with Oregano-Orange Chimichurri & Arugula Salad

Yield: 4 | Total Time: 15 Mins | Prep Time: 5 Mins | Cook Time: 10 Mins

Ingredients

- 1 teaspoon finely grated orange zest
- 1 teaspoon dried oregano
- 1 small garlic clove, grated
- 2 teaspoon vinegar (red wine, cider, or white wine)
- 1 tablespoon fresh orange juice
- 1/2 cup chopped fresh flat-leaf parsley leaves
- 1 ½ pound lean steak, cut into 4 pieces
- Sea salt and pepper
- 1/4 cup and 2 teaspoons extra virgin olive oil
- 4 cups arugula
- 2 bulbs fennel, shaved
- 2 tablespoons whole-grain mustard

Directions

1. Make chimichurri: In a medium bowl, combine orange zest, oregano and garlic. Mix in vinegar, orange juice and parsley and then slowly whisk in ¼ cup of olive oil until emulsified. Season with sea salt and pepper.
2. Sprinkle the steak with salt and pepper; heat the remaining olive oil in an instant pot and set on manual high; cook steak for about 6 Mins per side or until browned. Add water to an instant pot and insert a trivet; place beef over the trivet and lock lid. Cook on high for 10 Mins and then let pressure come down on its own. Let rest and slice.
3. Toss steak, greens, and fennel with mustard in a medium bowl; season with salt and pepper. Serve steak with chimichurri and salad. Enjoy!

Nutrition : Calories: 343; Total Fat: 20.6 g; Carbs: 2 g; Dietary Fiber: 0.5 g; Sugars: 0.8 g; Protein: 0.6 g; Cholesterol: 99 mg; Sodium: 146 mg

Instant Pot Paleo Meatballs

Yield: 4 | Total Time: 30 Mins | Prep Time: 15 Mins | Cook Time: 15 Mins

Ingredients

- 1 ½ pounds ground beef
- ¼ cups almond flour
- 2 beat eggs
- ⅔ cups diced red onion
- 5 teaspoons minced garlic
- ½ cups chopped basil
- ¾ cups tomato paste
- ½ cups grate carrot
- 2 cups dice tomato
- 1 teaspoon dried oregano
- 4 teaspoons minced garlic
- 1 teaspoon salt
- ½ cups water

Directions

1. In a bowl, mix garlic, basil leaves, tomato paste, and diced tomatoes.
2. In another bowl, mix together almond flour, garlic, carrot, onion, oregano, egg and salt until well blended; add ground beef and mix well. Roll out ¼ cup of the mixture into balls and brown them in an instant pot under sauté mode. Pour water and tomato mixture over the meat balls and lock lid. Cook on manual for 6 Mins and then let pressure come down on its own. Serve.

Nutrition : Calories: 417; Total Fat: 18 g; Carbs: 12 g; Dietary Fiber: 3 g; Sugars: 8 g; Protein: 43 g; Cholesterol: 214 mg; Sodium: 780 mg

Beef and Zucchini Lasagna

Yield:4 | Total Time: 48 Mins | Prep Time: 15 Mins | Cook Time: 33 Mins

Ingredients

- 1 large zucchini, spiralized into thin strips
- 1 cup marinara
- 16 oz. ground beef
- 10 oz. ricotta cheese
- 4 oz. shredded mozzarella cheese

Directions

1. Add water to your instant pot and insert a trivet. Sprinkle the zucchini noodles with salt and let sit for about 15 Mins. Brown the ground beef in a frying pan and stir in marinara, and salt and pepper.
2. In a casserole dish, layer the beef mixture, zucchini, ricotta cheese, tofu mixture, zucchini, ricotta cheese and top with mozzarella cheese; cover the dish with foil and place the dish on the trivet; lock lid and cook for 20 Mins and then quick release pressure. Uncover and broil for about 3 Mins or until the top is browned. Remove from oven and serve.

Nutrition : Calories: 456; Total Fat: 19.5 g; Carbs: 13.9 g; Dietary Fiber 2.5 g; Sugars: 7.2 g; Protein: 52.6 g; Cholesterol: 214 mg; Sodium: 780 mg

Instant Pot Barbacoa

Yield: 6 | Total Time: 1 Hour 10 Mins | Prep Time: 10 Mins

Ingredients

- 4 tablespoons olive oil
- 2 pounds grass-fed chuck roast, diced into large chunks
- 6 garlic cloves
- 1 large onion, chopped
- 2-4oz cans of green chilies
- 3 dried chipotle peppers, chopped
- 3 tbsp. coconut vinegar
- 1 cup fresh lime juice
- 1/2 cup water
- 1 tsp. salt
- 1 tsp. pepper
- 1 tbsp. cumin
- 1 tbsp. oregano

Directions

1. Combine all ingredients in your instant pot; lock lid and cook on high for 60 Mins. When done, release pressure naturally and shred before serving.

Nutrition : Calories: 276; Total Fat: 25.2 g; Carbs: 11 g; Dietary Fiber: 3.3 g; Sugars: 8.1 g; Protein: 23.9 g; Cholesterol: 60 mg; Sodium: 421 mg

Pressure Cooked Italian Beef

Yield: 6 | Total Time: 1 Hours 40 Mins | Prep Time: 10 Mins | Cook Time: 1 Hour 30 Mins

Ingredients

- 2 pound grass-fed chuck roast
- 6 cloves garlic
- 1 tsp. marjoram
- 1 tsp. basil
- 1 tsp. oregano
- 1/2 tsp. ground ginger
- 1 tsp. onion powder
- 2 tsp. garlic powder
- 1 tsp. salt
- 1/4 cup apple cider vinegar
- 1 cup beef broth

Directions

1. Cut slits in the roast with a sharp knife and then stuff with garlic cloves.
2. In a bowl, whisk together marjoram, basil, oregano, ground ginger, onion powder, garlic powder, and salt until well blended; rub the seasoning all over the roast and place it in your instant pot.
3. Add vinegar and broth and lock lid; cook on high for 90 Mins. Release pressure naturally and then shred meat with a fork.
4. Serve along with cooking juices.

Nutrition : Calories: 174; Total Fat: 9.2 g; Carbs: 1.9 g; Dietary Fiber: 0.3 g; Sugars: 0.4 g; Protein: 21 g; Cholesterol: 60 mg; Sodium: 487 mg

Roast Red Wine Beef Steak with Chili Olive Salsa

Yield: 6 | Total Time: 1 Hour 45 Mins | Prep Time: 15 Mins | Cook Time: 1 Hour 30 Mins

Ingredients

- 2kg leg of beef
- 2 tbsp. balsamic vinegar
- 3 red onions, each cut into 6 wedges
- 4 garlic cloves, sliced
- 3 cups hot lamb stock
- 2 tbsp. fresh lemon zest
- 8 good sprigs thyme
- ½ cup red wine
- 5 tbsp. extra virgin olive oil

Chili Olive Salsa

- 3 large tomatoes, finely chopped
- 1 cup olives, finely chopped
- 1 bird's eye chili, finely chopped
- Juice of 1 lemon
- ½ cup parsley, finely chopped

Directions

1. **Make salsa:** mix chopped tomato, olives, chili, lemon juice, and parsley in a large bowl.
2. With a knife, cut holes all over beef and push a garlic slice into each.
3. Mix lemon zest, wine, 3 tablespoons of olive oil, thyme and pepper in a freezer bag and add in the lamb, seal and refrigerate for about 4 hours or overnight.
4. Set your instant pot on manual high and heat oil; add in the remaining thyme and cook in steak for 5 Mins per side.
5. In the meantime, strain the marinade through a fine mesh into the pot. Lock lid and cook for 20 Mins and then naturally release pressure.
6. Transfer the steak to a cutting board and wrap in foil. Place onions in a bowl and set aside.
7. Set your instant pot to manual high and add in balsamic vinegar and a splash of stock; cook, scraping all the bits from the base and add to the jug with gravy. Serve the steak drizzled with the gravy.

Nutrition : Calories: 395; Total Fat: 17.8 g; Carbs: 5.3 g; Dietary Fiber: 0.9 g; Sugars: 2.5 g; Protein: 51.2 g; Cholesterol: 166 mg; Sodium: 242 mg

Instant Pot Chipotle Shredded Beef

Yield: 2 | Total Time: 1 Hour 30 Mins | Prep Time: 20 Mins | Cook Time: 1 Hour 10 Mins

Ingredients

- 2 tbsp. olive oil
- 2 pounds beef chuck roast
- 1 tbsp. adobo sauce
- 1 chipotle in adobo, chopped
- ½ tsp. chili powder
- 2 tsp. dried oregano
- 2 tsp. dried cumin
- 1 tsp. black pepper
- 2 tsp. salt
- 1 cup fresh cilantro, chopped
- 1 green bell pepper, diced
- 1 onion, chopped
- 1 cup water

Directions

1. Generously season the roast with salt and pepper.
2. Add olive oil to your instant pot and press the sauté button; add the roast and brown on both sides; spread adobo sauce and chipotle pepper over the roast and sprinkle with seasoning and cilantro; add bell pepper and onions and pour water around the edges of meat. Lock lid; cook on high for 60 Mins and then release pressure naturally.
3. Shred meat and serve with cooking sauce.

Nutrition : Calories: 665; Total Fat: 51.1 g; Carbs: 3.8 g; Dietary Fiber: 0.9 g; Sugars: 1.9 g; Protein: 45 g; Cholesterol: 175 mg; Sodium: 756 mg

Instant Pot AIP Beef

Yield: 6 | Total Time: 1 Hours 40 Mins | Prep Time: 10 Mins | Cook Time: 1 Hour 30 Mins

Ingredients

- 2 pound grass-fed chuck roast
- 6 cloves garlic
- 1 tsp. marjoram
- 1 tsp. basil
- 1 tsp. oregano
- 1/2 tsp. ground ginger
- 1 tsp. onion powder
- 2 tsp. garlic powder
- 1 tsp. salt
- 1/4 cup apple cider vinegar
- 1 cup beef broth

Directions

1. Cut slits in the roast with a sharp knife and then stuff with garlic cloves.
2. In a bowl, whisk together marjoram, basil, oregano, ground ginger, onion powder, garlic powder, and salt until well blended; rub the seasoning all over the roast and place it in your instant pot.
3. Add vinegar and broth and lock lid; cook on high for 90 Mins. Release pressure naturally and then shred meat with a fork.
4. Serve along with cooking juices.

Nutrition : Calories: 174; Total Fat: 9.2 g; Carbs: 1.9 g; Dietary Fiber: 0.3 g; Sugars: 0.4 g; Protein: 21 g; Cholesterol: 60 mg; Sodium: 487 mg

Beef & Sweet Potato Enchilada Casserole

Yield: 6 | Total Time: 40 Mins | Prep Time: 20 Mins | Cook Time: 20 Mins

Ingredients

- 2 small sweet potatoes
- 2 tablespoons olive oil
- 1-pound ground beef
- 1 can black beans, drained
- 1 cup frozen corn
- 1 can red enchilada sauce
- 4 tablespoon chopped fresh cilantro
- 2 teaspoon ground cumin
- 1 teaspoon garlic powder
- 1 teaspoon onion powder
- 1 small can diced olives
- 1 cup shredded parmesan cheese

Directions

1. Peel and cook the sweet potatoes; mash and mix with 2 tablespoons of cilantro.
2. In an instant pot set on manual high, cook the ground beef until browned. Stir in beans, corn, sauce and spices until well combined; sprinkle with half of the cheese and top with sweet potatoes, olives and cilantro. Cover with the remaining cheese and lock lid. Cook on high for 20 Mins and then let pressure come down on its own.

Nutrition : Calories: 315; Total Fat: 18.2 g; Carbs: 13.9 g; Dietary Fiber: 12.5 g; Sugars: 3.2 g; Protein: 31.6 g; Cholesterol: 54 mg; Sodium: 172 mg

Instant Pot Beef Roast

Yield: 6 | Total Time: 1 Hour 30 Mins | Prep Time: 20 Mins | Cook Time: 1 Hour 10 Mins

Ingredients

- 2 tbsp. olive oil
- 2 pounds beef chuck roast
- 1 tbsp. adobo sauce
- 1 chipotle in adobo, chopped
- ½ tsp. chili powder
- 2 tsp. dried oregano
- 2 tsp. dried cumin
- 1 tsp. black pepper
- 2 tsp. salt
- 1 cup fresh cilantro, chopped
- 1 green bell pepper, diced
- 1 onion, chopped
- 1 cup water

Directions

1. Generously season the roast with salt and pepper.
2. Add olive oil to your instant pot and press the sauté button; add the roast and brown on both sides; spread adobo sauce and chipotle pepper over the roast and sprinkle with seasoning and cilantro; add bell pepper and onions and pour water around the edges of meat. Lock lid; cook on high for 60 Mins and then release pressure naturally.
3. Shred meat and serve with cooking sauce.

Nutrition : Calories: 665; Total Fat: 51.1 g; Carbs: 3.8 g; Dietary Fiber: 0.9 g; Sugars: 1.9 g; Protein: 45 g; Cholesterol: 175 mg; Sodium: 756 mg

Paleo Instant Pot Beef Jalapeno Chili

Yield: 2 | Total Time: 1 Hour 55 Mins | Prep Time: 25 Mins | Cook Time: 1 Hour 30 Mins

Ingredients

- 2 tablespoons olive oil
- 1/2 pound ground beef
- 1 red bell pepper, chopped
- 1 green bell pepper, chopped
- 2 jalapeños, finely diced
- 1/2 acorn squash, diced
- 1 zucchini, sliced
- 2 small carrots, sliced
- 2 green onions, thinly sliced
- 1 cup canned tomatoes
- 4 tbsp. chili powder
- 4 tbsp. tomato paste
- 4 tbsp. can tomato sauce

Directions

1. Set your instant pot on manual high and heat oil; brown ground beef and then stir in, bell peppers, jalapeños, zucchinis, carrots, onions, and squash. Add whole tomatoes and stir with a spatula to mix well. Stir in chili powder along with the remaining ingredients and lock lid. Cook on high for 1 ½ hours and then release the pressure naturally.

Nutritional Information Per Serving
Calories: 120; Total Fat: 11.6 g; Carbs: 1.9 g; Dietary fiber: 0.6 g; Sugars: 0.3 g; Protein: 2.9 g; Cholesterol: 20 mg; Sodium: 163 mg

Low Carb Cheese Steak Casserole with Fresh Lemon Juice

Yield: 6 | Total Time 50 Mins | Prep Time 5 Mins | Cook Time 45 Mins

Ingredients

- 4 tablespoons olive oil
- 1 ½ pounds lean ground beef
- 1 clove garlic
- 1/2 yellow onion
- 2 bell peppers
- 4 slices Provolone cheese
- 1 teaspoon Worcestershire sauce
- 1 teaspoon hot sauce
- 1/4 cup heavy cream
- 4 large eggs
- 1 teaspoon seasoned salt
- 6 glasses freshly squeezed lemon juice

Directions

1. Set your instant pot on manual high and heat oil; add in beef and cook, crumbling; stir in garlic, onion, peppers and salt. Cook until beef is browned. Top with cheese pieces. In a bowl, whisk together cream, egg, Worcestershire sauce and hot sauce until well blended; pour over the beef mixture and lock lid. Cook on high for 15 Mins and then let pressure come down naturally. Serve with a glass of freshly squeezed lemon juice.

Nutrition : Calories: 366; Fat: 34g; Carbs: 5g; Protein: 23g

Tasty Lime Steak with Green Salad

Yield: 6 | Total Time: 20 Mins | Prep Time: 10 Mins | Cook Time: 10 Mins

Ingredients

- 1-pound flank steak
- 3 tbsp. toasted sesame oil
- 1 tsp. hot pepper sauce
- 2 tbsp. fresh lime juice
- 1 garlic clove, chopped
- 6 scallions, thinly sliced
- 3 tbsp. olive oil
- 1/3 cup soy sauce
- 1 tsp liquid Stevia
- Kosher salt
- 4 cups green salad

Directions

1. In a resealable plastic bag, combine scallions, garlic, lime juice, olive oil, sesame oil, Stevia, and soy sauce; add steak and seal the bag. Shake to coat the steak well and refrigerate for at least 8 hours.
2. Add oil to an instant pot and set to manual high; remove steak from the bag and shake off excess marinade; season with salt and fry the meat for about 6 Mins per side or until browned. Remove meat from the pot and add in water; insert a metal trivet and place the beef on it. Lock lid and cook on high for 10 Mins. Let pressure come down.
3. Transfer the steak to a chopping board and let rest for at least 10 Mins; slice thinly and serve with green salad.

Nutrition : Calories: 251; Fat: 17.6g; Carbs: 4.9g; Protein: 19g

Loaded Low Carb Flank Steak with Steamed Asian Veggies

Yield: 6 | Total Time: 30 Mins | Prep Time: 15 Mins | Cook Time: 15Mins

Ingredients

- 2 pounds beef flank steak
- 1/2 cup softened butter
- 2 tbsp. salad dressing mix
- 3 green onions, chopped

Steamed Asian Veggies
- 1 bunch broccoli, trimmed
- 1 bunch baby choy sum, trimmed

- 6 cooked and crumbled bacon strips
- 1/2 tsp. pepper

- 1/2 tsp. sesame seeds, toasted

Directions

1. **Prepare Veggies:** Separate the leaves from the stems of choy sum. Place a steamer over a large saucepan or wok of simmering water; place broccoli and choy sum stems in the steamer and cover. Cook for about 4 Mins or until tender; add the choy sum leaves and continue cooking, covered, for about 2 Mins or until wilted.
2. Beat butter, salad dressing mix, onions, bacon strips, and pepper in a small bowl. Horizontally cut a small pocket in the steak and fill with the butter mixture.
3. Add oil to an instant pot and set to manual high; fry in the meat for about 7 Mins per side or until browned. Remove meat from the pot and add in water; insert a metal trivet and place the beef on it. Lock lid and cook on high for 10 Mins. Let pressure come down.
4. Transfer to a chopping board and slice across the grain. Serve.

Nutrition : Calories: 493; Fat: 36.9g; Carbs: 2.6g; Protein: 36.5g

Beef Stir Fry with Red Onions & Cabbage

Yield: 4 | Total Time: 20 Mins | Prep Time: 10 Mins | Cook Time: 10 Mins

Ingredients:

- 550g grass-fed flank steak, thinly sliced strips
- 1 tablespoon rice wine
- 2 teaspoons balsamic vinegar
- Pinch of sea salt
- Pinch of pepper
- 4 tablespoons extra-virgin olive oil
- 1 large yellow onion, thinly chopped
- 1/2 red bell pepper, thinly sliced
- 1/2 green bell pepper, thinly sliced
- 1 tablespoon toasted sesame seeds
- 1 teaspoon crushed red pepper flakes
- 4 cups cabbage
- 1 ½ avocados, diced

Directions:

1. Place meat in a bowl; stir in rice wine and vinegar, sea salt and pepper. Toss to coat well.
2. Heat a tablespoon of olive oil in an instant pot set on manual high; add meat and cook for about 2 Mins or until meat is browned; stir for another 2 Mins and then remove from heat. Sauté the onions for about 2 Mins or until caramelized; stir in pepper and cook for 2 Mins more. Stir in cabbage and cook for 2 Mins; stir in sesame seeds and red pepper flakes. Lock lid and cook for 5 Mins on high setting. Let pressure come down on its own. Serve hot topped with diced avocado!

Nutrition : Calories: 459; Fat: 30g; Carbs: 16.6g; Protein: 35.3g

Chili Fried Steak with Toasted Cashews & Sautéed Spinach

Yields: 4 | Total Time: 35 Mins | Prep Time: 10 Mins | Cook Time: 25 Mins

Ingredients

- 3 tbsp. extra virgin olive oil or canola oil
- 1 pound sliced lean beef
- 2 tablespoons apple cider vinegar
- 2 teaspoon fish sauce
- 2 teaspoons red curry paste
- 1 cup green capsicum, diced
- 24 toasted cashews
- 1 teaspoon arrowroot
- 1 teaspoon liquid Stevia
- ½ cup water
- 2 cups spinach
- 1 tablespoon butter
- 1 red onion, chopped

Directions

1. Prepare spinach: melt butter in a skillet and sauté onion until fragrant; stir in kale for 3 Mins or until wilted.
2. Add oil to an instant pot set on manual high; add beef and fry until it is no longer pink inside. Stir in red curry paste and cook for a few more Mins.
3. Stir in Stevia, vinegar, fish sauce, capsicum and water. Lock lid and cook on high for 10 Mins. Naturally release the pressure.
4. Mix cooked arrowroot with water to make a paste; stir the paste into the sauce and cook on manual high until the sauce is thick. Stir in toasted cashews and serve with sautéed spinach.

Nutrition : Calories: 346; Fat: 14.1g; Carbs: 7.9g; Protein: 26.4g

Protein-Rich Beef & Veggie Stew

Yield: 4 | Total Time: 3 Hours 10 Mins | Prep Time: 10 Mins | Cook Time: 3 Hours

Ingredients

- 2 cups zucchini, cubed
- 2 lb. beef (chuck), cubed
- 1 cup eggplant, cubed
- 1 can tomato sauce
- 1/2 cup onion, chopped
- 4 tbsp. extra virgin olive oil
- 1 clove garlic, chopped
- ½ cup vegetable broth
- 1 carrot, thinly sliced
- 1 tomato, chopped
- ¼ tsp paprika
- ½ tsp Cumin, ground
- ½ tsp turmeric, ground
- ¼ tsp cinnamon, ground
- ¼ tsp red pepper, crushed

Directions

1. Combine everything in an instant pot, cover and cook on high for 3 hours. Let pressure come down on its own. Serve with steamed cauliflower rice.
2. Enjoy!

Nutrition : Calories: 301; Fat: 20.3g; Carbs: 6.9g; Protein: 24.4g

Peppered Steak with Cherry Tomatoes

Yield: 4 | Total Time: 25 Mins | Prep Time: 10 Mins | Cook Time: 10 Mins

Ingredients

- 4 (250g each) beef sirloin steaks, trimmed
- 4 tbsp. extra virgin olive oil
- 2 tsp. cracked black pepper
- 1 bunch rocket, trimmed
- 2 cups cherry tomatoes
- 4 cups green salad, to serve
- olive oil cooking spray

Directions

1. Brush the steak with oil. Place the pepper on a large plate and press the steaks into the pepper until well coated.
2. Set your instant pot to manual high; add oil and heat. Add in steaks and cook for 5 Mins per side. Lock lid and cook on high for 3 Mins and the let pressure come down on its own.
3. In the meantime, spray the tomatoes with oil and barbecue them, turning occasionally, for about 5 Mins or until tender.
4. Arrange the rocket on serving plates and add steaks and tomatoes; serve with green salad.

Nutrition : Calories: 625; Fat: 41.8g (60%); Carbs: 6.5g (4%); Protein: 54.2g (36%)

Keto Ground Beef Chili served with Avocado

Yield: 1 Serving | Total Time: 25 Mins | Prep Time: 10 Mins | Cook Time: 15 Mins

Ingredients

- 180 grams lean ground beef
- 1 ½ tablespoons olive oil
- 1 tablespoon chopped red onion
- 2 cloves garlic, minced
- 1 cup chopped tomatoes
- ½ cup water
- Pinch of garlic powder
- ¼ teaspoon chili powder
- Pinch of oregano
- Pinch of onion powder
- Pinch of cayenne pepper
- Pinch of salt
- Pinch of pepper
- ¼ avocado, chopped tomato and green onion to serve

Directions:

1. Set your instant pot on manual high setting, cook beef in olive oil until browned; stir in garlic, onion, tomatoes, water and spices. Lock lid and cook on high setting for 10 Mins and then let pressure come down naturally. Season with salt and pepper. Serve topped with diced avocado, chopped tomato and green onion.

Nutrition : Calories: 558; Fat: 37.4g; Carbs: 17.84g; Protein: 42.3g

Loaded Flank Steak with Salsa

Yield: 1 Serving | Total Time: 34 Mins | Prep Time: 10 Mins | Cook Time: 24 Mins

Ingredients

- 150g beef flank steak
- 1 tablespoon softened butter
- 2 tbsp. salad dressing mix
- 3 green onions, chopped
- 1 cooked and crumbled bacon strip
- 1/2 tsp. pepper
- ½ cup broth

For the salsa

- 1 large tomato, finely chopped
- 1 tablespoon capers, finely chopped
- 1 bird's eye chili, finely chopped
- Juice of 1/4 lemon
- ½ cup parsley, finely chopped

Directions

1. Make salsa: mix chopped tomato, capers, chili, lemon juice, and parsley in a large bowl.
2. Beat butter, salad dressing mix, onions, bacon strips, and pepper in a small bowl. Horizontally cut a small pocket in the steak and fill with the butter mixture.
3. Set your instant pot on manual high; heat oil and fry the steak for about 7 Mins per side or until well cooked. Add in broth and lock lid. Cook on high setting for 10 Mins and then let pressure come down naturally. Transfer to a chopping board and slice across the grain. Serve with salsa.

Nutrition : Calories: 545; Total Fat: 30.3 g; Carbs: 14.9 g; Dietary fiber: 4.9 g; Sugars: 6.1 g; Protein: 58.7 g; Cholesterol: 185 mg; Sodium: 1289 mg

Instant Pot Beef & Zucchini

Yield: 1 Serving | Total Time: 25 Mins | Prep Time: 10 Mins | Cook Time: 15 Mins

Ingredients

- 100g lean ground beef
- 1 medium zucchini, diced
- 1 tbsp. coconut oil
- 1/2 yellow onion, diced
- 1-2 cloves garlic, minced
- 2 medium tomatoes, diced
- 2 tbsp. dried oregano

Directions

1. Rinse and prepare the veggies.
2. Set your instant pot and melt coconut oil; stir in onions and sauté for about 4 Mins or until translucent.
3. Roll ground beef into small balls and add to the pot along with oregano and garlic; cook for about 5 Mins. Add tomatoes and zucchini and lock lid. Cook on high for 3 Mins and then let pressure come down on its own.
4. Serve and enjoy!

Nutrition : Calories: 423; Total Fat: 28.1 g; Carbs: 13.8 g; Dietary fiber: 4.9 g; Sugars: 5.7 g; Protein: 30.7 g; Cholesterol: 99 mg; Sodium: 189 mg

Coriander & Buttermilk Steak with Salad

Yield: 6 | Total Time: 25 Mins | Prep Time: 15 Mins | Cook Time: 10 Mins

Ingredients

- 4 tbsp. extra virgin olive oil
- 2 cups buttermilk
- 3 lb. beef skirt steak
- 3 cloves garlic, chopped
- 1 lime, zested, juiced
- 1 long green chilli, sliced
- 1 bunch coriander, chopped
- 3 cucumbers, cut into wedges
- 1 bunch radish, quartered
- 3 avocados, diced
- baby lettuce, outer leaves removed

Directions

1. In a food processor, combine garlic, zest, chili, and coriander; pulse to a coarse paste; add buttermilk and continue pulsing until well combined. Reserve a cup of the dressing.
2. Place the steak in a bowl; pour over the remaining dressing. Refrigerate, covered, for about 1 hour.
3. Set your instant pot to manual high; add oil and heat. Remove the steak from the marinade and brush with oil. Add in steaks and cook for 5 Mins per side. Lock lid and cook on high for 3 Mins and the let pressure come down on its own.
4. Slice the steak into thin strips and serve with the salad, drizzled with the buttermilk dressing.
5. Divide the lettuce leaves and place in a bowl; add radishes, cucumber and avocado.
6. Whisk lime juice, salt and pepper into the reversed dressing.

Nutrition : Calories: 523; Fat: 35.8g; Carbs: 14.1g; Protein: 40.1g

Cheese Stuffed Meatloaf Stuffed

Yield: 6 | Total Time: 50 Mins | Prep Time: 5 Mins | Cook Time: 45 Mins

Ingredients

- 1 egg
- 1-pound ground Chorizo
- 1-pound ground beef
- 1/2 cup coconut flour
- 2 garlic cloves, minced
- 1/4 red onion, minced
- 1/2 tablespoon smoked paprika
- 1/2 tablespoon onion powder
- 1/2 tablespoon garlic powder
- ¾ cup sliced cheddar cheese
- 1/2 teaspoon salt
- 1/2 teaspoon pepper
- 6 cups tomato salsa

Directions

1. In a large bowl, mix all ingredients except salsa and cheese. Press half of the meat mixture in a loaf pan that fits into your instant pot; top with cheese and add the remaining meat mixture, pressing it down to slightly compress. Add water to your instant pot and insert a trivet. Place the dish over the trivet and lock lid. Cook on high for 45 Mins and then let pressure come down naturally. Let rest for at least 10 Mins before serving.
2. Serve the meatloaf with salsa.

Nutrition : Calories: 602; Total Fat: 40.2 g; Carbs: 10.5 g; Dietary fiber: 4.5 g; Sugars: 0.8 g; Protein: 47.3 g; Cholesterol: 176 mg; Sodium: 1276 mg

INSTANT POT KETO PORK RECIPES

Feta & Spinach Stuffed Pork

Yield: 4 | Total Time: 30 Mins | Prep Time: 10 Mins | Cook Time: 20 Mins

Ingredients

- 4 (6-ounce) pork chops, butterflied
- 1 /3 cup crumbled feta
- 1 /2 cup frozen spinach
- 2 tablespoons coconut oil
- 1 /4 teaspoon dried parsley
- 1 /4 teaspoon dried oregano
- 1 /4 teaspoon garlic powder
- 1 cup water
- 1 /4 teaspoon pepper
- 11 /4 teaspoons salt, divided

Directions

1. Pound the pork chops to ¼-inch thickness. In a large bowl, mix together feta cheese, spinach and salt; divide the mixture onto the pork chops and close the chops with butcher's string or toothpicks. Set your instant pot on sauté mode and heat coconut oil; sear the pork chops for about 7 Mins per side or until golden browned. Press the cancel button.
2. Remove the pork chops and pour in water; insert a metal trivet and place the chops on the trivet. Lock lid and cook on high for 15 Mins. Quick release the pressure and then serve chops with favorite low carb sauce.

Nutrition : Calories: 301; Total Fat: 11.8 g; Carbs: 1.6 g; Dietary Fiber: 0.7 g; Sugars: 0.7 g; Protein: 40.8 g; Cholesterol: 62 mg; Sodium: 931 mg

Pressure Cooked Sour Cream Pork Chops

Yield: 4 | Total Time: 30 Mins | Prep Time: 10 Mins | Cook Time: 20 Mins

Ingredients

- 4 boneless pork chops
- 2 medium onions, chopped
- 1 coconut oil
- 1/3 cup sour cream
- 1 teaspoon arrowroot
- 1 teaspoon Worcestershire sauce
- 1 cup beef stock
- salt and pepper

Directions

1. Set your instant pot on sauté mode and heat in oil; sauté onions until tender. Add in pork chops and stir in salt and pepper. Switch to the pot and then stir in Worcestershire sauce and beef stock. Lock lid and cook on high for 8 Mins and then let pressure come down on its own.
2. Set the pot on simmer and stir in a mix of arrowroot and water. Cook for 5 Mins and then stir in sour cream. Serve hot.

Nutrition : Calories: 360; Total Fat: 27.7 g; Carbs: 6.3 g; Dietary Fiber: 1.2 g; Sugars: 2.6 g; Protein: 20.6g; Cholesterol: 87 mg; Sodium: 280 mg

Four-Ingredient Pork Chops

Yield: 4 | Total Time: 20 Mins | Prep Time: 10 Mins | Cook Time: 10 Mins

Ingredients

- 4 medium pork chops
- 2 tablespoons olive oil
- 1/2 cup water
- 2 tablespoons BBQ sauce

Directions

1. Set your instant pot on sauté mode and heat in oil; brown in the meat and transfer to a plate.
2. Stir in water and then add in BBQ sauce; return the meat and lock lid. Cook on high for 5 Mins and the let pressure come down on its own.
3. Serve hot.

Nutritional Information per Serving:

Calories: 308; Total Fat: 17 g; Carbs: 7 g; Dietary Fiber: 2 g; Sugars: 3 g; Protein: 30g; Cholesterol: 89 mg; Sodium: 1153 mg

Instant Pot Low Lime Carb Pork Carnitas

Yield: 4 | Total Time: 1 Hour 40 Mins | Prep Time: 10 Mins | Cook Time: 1 Hour 10 Mins

Ingredients

- 2 tablespoons olive oil
- 4 pounds boneless pork shoulder, diced
- 4 garlic cloves diced
- 1/2 onion diced
- 1 jalapeño pepper, chopped
- 1/2 cup chicken stock
- 1 tablespoon orange zest
- 2 tablespoons fresh orange juice
- 2 tablespoons lime zest
- ½ cup fresh lime juice
- 1/2 teaspoon dried oregano
- 2 teaspoons smoked paprika
- 2 teaspoons ground cumin
- 1 dried bay leaf
- salt and pepper

Directions

1. Set your instant pot on sauté mode and heat oil; brown the meat and transfer to a plate. Add onions, salt and pepper to the pot and cook for 2 Mins and then stir in garlic for 20 seconds.
2. Stir in the remaining ingredients and return the pork meat. Lock lid and cook on high for 90 Mins. Let pressure come down on its own.
3. Serve the pork in lettuce leaves drizzled with lime juice. Enjoy!

Nutrition : Calories: 312; Total Fat: 14 g; Carbs: 2.7 g; Dietary Fiber: 2 g; Sugars: 1 g; Protein: 41g; Cholesterol: 123 mg; Sodium: 992 mg

Low Carb Pork Tenderloin

Yield: 4 | Total Time: 35 Mins | Prep Time; 10 Mins | Cook Time: 25 Mins

Ingredients:

- 4 tablespoons olive oil, divided
- 6 cloves garlic
- 1 ½ pounds pork tenderloin
- ½ teaspoon Italian herbs
- 1 teaspoon salt
- ½ teaspoon pepper
- 1 head broccoli
- 1 medium onion

Directions

1. Set your instant pot on manual high. Poke holes all over pork tenderloin with a folk; stuff the holes with minced garlic and rub the pork with a tablespoon of olive oil, herbs, salt and pepper. Heat another tablespoon of olive oil in the pot and then add the pork tenderloin; cook for about 6 Mins or until browned on all sides. Add in the remaining oil and then stir in onions and broccoli. Lock lid and cook on high for 20 Mins. Let pressure come down on its own.
2. Remove the pork from the pot and let rest for at least 10 Mins before serving.

Nutrition : Calories: 267; Fat: 16.7g; Carbs: 4.6g; Protein: 18.6g

Pressure Cooked Parmesan Dijon Crusted Pork Chops

Yield: 4 | Total Time: 45 Mins | Prep Time: 15 Mins | Cook Time: 30 Mins

Ingredients

- 4 boneless pork loin chops
- 2 tablespoons olive oil
- 1/4 teaspoon Italian seasoning
- 2 tablespoons spiced brown mustard
- 1/4 cup Dijon mustard
- 1/4 teaspoon dried oregano
- 1/4 teaspoon onion powder
- 1/2 teaspoon dried thyme
- 1/2 teaspoon garlic powder
- 1/4 teaspoon dried basil
- 1/4 teaspoon sea salt
- 1/4 teaspoon black pepper
- 1 cup grated Parmesan cheese
- 4 cups kale, chopped
- 2 tablespoons butter
- 2 red onions

Directions

1. Rub the pork chops with sea salt and pepper. In a bowl, mix together olive oil, spicy brown mustard, Italian seasoning, Dijon mustard, oregano, onion powder, thyme, garlic powder, and basil. Dust the pork chops with the spice mixture until well coated.
2. Set your instant pot on manual high; add oil and cook in the pork chops for 5 Mins per side. Add water to the pot and insert a metal trivet.
3. Spread cheese in a single layer on a plate; coat the chops generously with the cheese. Arrange the chops on aluminum foil and place over the trivet. Lock the pot and cook on high for 20 Mins and then quick release the pressure. Transfer the pork to the oven and broil on high for about 5 Mins or until crispy and golden brown.
4. Meanwhile, heat butter in a skillet over medium heat; sauté onions until fragrant and stir in kale. Cook for 3 Mins or until wilted. Serve the pork chops with sautéed kale.

Nutrition : Calories: 346; Fat: 24.2; Carbs: 2.6g; Protein: 34g

Instant Pot Pork Chops with Steamed Veggies & Creamy Sesame Dressing

Yield: 6 | Total Time: 20 Mins | Prep Time: 5 Mins | Cook Time: 15 Mins

Ingredients

- 2 tablespoons olive oil
- 1.5 pounds boneless pork chops
- 2 garlic cloves minced
- 1/2 medium onion sliced
- 1 tablespoon Italian seasoning
- 1/2 cup cheddar cheese
- 1/3 cup parmesan cheese
- 1 oz. cream cheese
- 1 cup heavy whipping cream
- 1/3 cup chicken broth
- 1/2 teaspoon pepper
- 1/2 teaspoon salt

Steamed Sesame Greens

- 1 bunch broccoli, ends trimmed
- 1 bunch asparagus, trimmed
- 1 bunch choy sum, ends trimmed
- 2 cups water

Dressing

- 1 tbsp. toasted sesame seeds
- 1/2 tsp. sesame oil
- 1 tbsp. raw honey
- 2 tbsp. oyster sauce
- 2 small garlic cloves, crushed
- 2 tbsp. extra virgin olive oil

Directions

1. **Prepare the Veggies:** Add water to a wok set over high heat; cover and bring to a rolling boil. Add the veggies to a steamer and cover with lid; place over the wok and steam for about 5 Mins or until tender.
2. **Make dressing:** In a screw-top jar, combine the dressing ingredients; shake well. Serve the steamed veggies onto serving plate and pour over each serving the dressing; toss to coat well and serve.
3. **Prepare the Meat:** Heat two tablespoons of olive oil in an instant pot; brown onion, garlic and pork chops for about 5 Mins; transfer the pork chops to a plate and add the remaining ingredients to the pot and cook on medium until the sauce is thick. Return the chops and lock lid. Cook on high for 10 Mins and then quick release the pressure by pressing venting button.
4. Serve the pork chops with steamed veggies drizzled with the dressing. Yummy!

Nutrition : Calories: 438; Fat: 33.2g; Carbs: 2.7g; Protein: 30.1g

Shredded Pressure-Cooked Pork with Green Salad and Avocado

Yield: 6 | Total Time: 2 Hours 10 Mins | Prep Time: 10 Mins | Cook Time: 2 Hours

Ingredients

- 1/4 cup butter
- 3 pounds pork roast
- 2 cups chicken stock
- 1 batch taco seasoning
- 8 cups green salad
- 2 avocados, diced

Directions

1. Set your instant pot on manual high and melt butter; brown pork roast and add in chicken stock and taco seasoning; lock lid and cook on high for 2 hours. Let pressure come down on its own. When ready, shred the meat with fork. Serve with green salad topped with diced avocado.

Nutrition : Calories: 438; Fat: 17.8g; Carbs: 9.7g; Protein: 23.1g

Instant Pot Pork Chops with Bacon & Caramelized Onions

Yield: 4 | Total Time: 50 Mins | Prep Time: 10 Mins | Cook Time: 40 Mins

Ingredients

- 4 large boneless pork chops
- 4 slices bacon, diced
- 4 tablespoons butter
- 1 large onion, sliced
- salt and pepper to taste
- 1/2 cup chicken broth
- 1/4 cup heavy cream
- 1 tablespoon water
- 1 teaspoon arrowroot

Directions

1. Set your instant pot on manual high; add bacon and cook until crispy; transfer to a plate and keep warm. Add butter to the pot and sauté onions until fragrant; stir in salt and cook onions until caramelized. Transfer the onions to another plate and keep warm.
2. Sprinkle the pork chops with sea salt and pepper; add to pot and cook for about 3 Mins per side.
3. In a bowl, stir together arrowroot powder and water; whisk in cream and chicken broth until smooth. Add to the pork chops and lock lid. Cook on high for 20 Mins and then quick release the pressure. Top with bacon and caramelized onions and cook on manual high for about 10 Mins. Serve hot!

Nutrition : Calories: 585; Fat: 40.4g; Carbs: 4.9g; Protein: 48.6g

Instant Pot BBQ Pork Wraps

Yield: 2 | Total Time: 2 Hours 15 Mins | Prep Time: 15 Mins | Cook Time: 2 Hours

Ingredients

- 2 (200-gram) boneless pork ribs
- 1 1/2 cups beef broth
- 2 tbsp. barbeque sauce
- 4 lettuce leaves

Directions

1. Combine pork ribs and bone broth in your instant pot and cook on high setting for 1 ½ hours. Let pressure come down naturally. Shred pork and transfer to a baking dish; stir in barbecue sauce and bake at 350°F for about 30 Mins. Divide the pork among lettuce leaves and roll to form wraps. Serve.

Nutrition : Calories: 294; Total Fat: 9.2 g; Carbs: 4.6 g; Dietary Fiber: 0.1 g; Sugars: 0.8 g; Protein: 18.2g; Cholesterol: 112 mg; Sodium: 347 mg

Pork & Mushroom Dumplings

Yield: 6 | Total Time: 12 Mins | Prep Time: 10 Mins | Cook Time: 2 Mins

Ingredients

- 1 ¾ pounds ground pork
- 1 egg, beaten
- 3 tbsp. sesame oil
- 4 tbsp. soy sauce
- 2 tbsp. sliced green onion
- 4 cloves garlic, minced
- 1 cup mushrooms, minced
- 1 tbsp. minced ginger
- 100 wonton wrappers, sliced into circles
- Sliced green onions

Directions

1. In a bowl, mix together pork, egg, sesame oil, soy sauce, green onion, ginger, and garlic until well combined.
2. Lay down the wonton wrapper and wet the edges; add three teaspoons of the mixture in the center and roll up to wrap.
3. Insert a steamer basket in your instant pot and add a cup of water; arrange the shumai in the basket in a single layer and then lock lid. Cook on manual high for 2 Mins. Let pressure come down naturally and then remove the shumai. Serve garnished with more green onions.

Nutrition : Calories: 93; Total Fat: 21.5 g; Carbs: 6.5 g; Dietary Fiber: 0 g; Sugars: 3 g; Protein: 11g; Cholesterol: Sodium: 347 mg

Instant Pot Low Carb Spiced Pork Chops

Yield: 4 | Total Time: 1 Hour 40 Mins | Prep Time: 10 Mins | Cook Time: 1 Hour 30 Mins

Ingredients

- 2 pounds pork chops
- 3 heads garlic, cut in half across
- 3 brown onions, cut into wedges
- 200g cauliflower
- 200g broccoli
- 200g green beans
- 1 pouch cheese sauce
- 2 tbsp. seasoning blend

Directions

1. Add water to an instant pot and insert a metal trivet.
2. On an aluminum foil, combine garlic and onion; sprinkle with olive oil.
3. Rub the pork chops seasoning blend into the pork and place it on top of the bed of garlic and onion; fold the foil to wrap the contents and place over the trivet. Lock lid and cook on high for 90 Mins. Release pressure naturally.
4. Transfer the chops to the oven and broil for about 20 Mins or until browned and crisp on the outside.

Nutrition : Calories: 665; Fat: 46.6g; Carbs: 11.2g; Protein: 49.1g

Barbecued Pork Chops with Broccoli

Yield: 4 | Total Time: 1 Hour 5 Mins | Prep Time: 10 Mins | Cook Time: 55 Mins

Ingredients

- 1 tsp. bottled BBQ sauce
- ½ tsp. garlic powder
- 4 pork chops, 1-inch thick
- 1 cup non-fat milk
- Salt and pepper
- 5 cups frozen broccoli florets (450g)

Directions

1. Generously sprinkle pork chops with BBQ sauce and garlic powder. Set your instant pot on manual high and add in the pork chops, cook turning once, for about 10 Mins or until cooked through. Add in milk and lock lid. Cook on high for 30 Mins and then quick release the pressure.
2. Place broccoli in a microwave-safe pot and cover; microwave on high for about 5 Mins; remove from heat and let stand. Microwave again for 2 Mins and serve with the pork chops.

Nutrition : Calories: 353; Total Fat: 39g; Carbs: 7.8g; Protein: 13g

Keto Bone-In Pork Chops

Yield: 6 | Total Time: 35 Mins | Prep Time: 15 Mins | Cook Time: 20 Mins

Ingredients

- 3 ¾ inch thick bone-in pork chops
- 3 russet potatoes
- 1/4 cup butter,
- 3 tbsp. Worcestershire sauce
- 1 cup vegetable broth
- 1 onion, chopped
- 1 cup baby carrots
- Salt & pepper

Directions

1. Season the pork chops with salt and pepper.
2. Melt two tablespoons of butter in your instant pot set on sauté mode; brown the pork chops in batches and then transfer to a platter.
3. Add the remaining butter to the pot and cook onion and carrots for about 2 Mins; stir in Worcestershire sauce and then add in the pork chops. Add potatoes in a steamer basket and place it in the pot; lock lid and cook on high for 13 Mins. Let pressure come down naturally and then slice the potatoes. Serve with pork chops.

Nutrition : Calories: 345; Total Fat: 19.8 g; Carbs: 11.2 g; Dietary Fiber: 0.3 g; Sugars: 3.4 g; Protein: 21.1g; Cholesterol: 220 mg; Sodium: 912 mg

Pork Roast w/ Cauliflower Gravy

Yield: 6 | Total Time: 1 Hour 45 Mins | Prep Time: 15 Mins | Cook Time: 1 Hour 30 Mins

Ingredients

- 3-pound pork roast
- 4 cloves garlic
- 1 red onion, chopped
- 4 cups chopped cauliflower
- 2 ribs celery
- 2 tbsp. organic coconut oil
- 1 cup sliced portabella mushrooms
- 1 tsp. sea salt
- ½ tsp. black pepper
- 2 cups filtered water

Directions

1. Add garlic, onion, cauliflower, water and celery to your instant pot; add pork and season with salt and pepper; lock lid and cook on high for 1 hour and then let pressure come down on own.
2. Transfer pork to a baking dish and bake at 400°F for about 15 Mins.
3. Meanwhile, transfer cooked veggies along with broth to a blender and blend until very smooth.
4. Add coconut oil to your pot and set on sauté mode; add mushrooms and cook for about 5 Mins or until tender; stir in veggie puree and cook until thick.
5. Serve shredded pork with mushroom gravy.

Nutrition : Calories: 393; Total Fat: 21.5 g; Carbs: 13.5 g; Dietary Fiber: 0.9g; Sugars: 5.4 g; Protein: 18.1g; Cholesterol: 292 Sodium: 347 mg

Italian Pulled Pork Ragu

Yield: 6 | Total Time: 1 Hour | Prep Time: 10 Mins | Cook Time: 50 Mins

Ingredients:

- 1 pound pork tenderloin
- 1 tsp. kosher salt
- black pepper, to taste
- 4 tablespoons olive oil
- 5 cloves garlic, minced
- 4 cups crushed tomatoes
- 1 cup roasted red peppers
- 2 sprigs fresh thyme
- 2 bay leaves
- 1 tbsp. chopped fresh parsley, divided

Directions:

1. Season the pork with salt and pepper.
2. Set your instant pot on sauté mode and add oil; sauté garlic for about two Mins until tender and then add pork; brown for about two Mins per side and then stir in the remaining ingredients.
3. Lock lid and cook on high for 45 Mins. Release the pressure naturally and serve.

Nutrition : Calories: 93; Total Fat: 21.5 g; Carbs: 6.5 g; Dietary Fiber: 0 g; Sugars: 3 g; Protein: 11g; Cholesterol: Sodium: 347 mg

Instant Pot Herbed Pork

Yield: 4 | Total Time: 45 Mins | Prep Time: 10 Mins | Cook Time: 35 Mins

Ingredients

- 8 pork chops
- 2 Italian sausages removed from casings
- 1 medium red bell pepper, diced
- 1 small onion, thinly sliced
- 4 cloves garlic, pressed
- 2 tablespoons dry vermouth
- ¼ cup fresh parsley, chopped
- 1 teaspoon corn starch
- ¼ tsp coarsely ground pepper
- ½ tsp dried oregano
- 2 tsps. dried rosemary
- 2 tbsp. cold water
- Salt

Directions

1. Combine onion, garlic, bell pepper, rosemary and oregano in your instant pot. Crumble the sausages over the mixture, casings removed. Arrange the pork in a single layer over the sausage and sprinkle with pepper. Add the vermouth and lock lid; cook on high for 30 Mins. Naturally release the pressure.
2. Move the pork to a warm, deep platter and cover.
3. Mix the corn starch with the water in a small bowl and add this to the liquid in the pot. Lock lid and cook on high for 2 Mins; season with salt. Pour the soup over the pork and garnish with parsley. Enjoy!

Nutrition : Calories: 284; Total Fat: 20.1 g; Carbs: 5.6g; Dietary Fiber: 1 g; Sugars: 2.3 g; Protein: 18.8 g; Cholesterol: 69 mg; Sodium: 99 mg

Pressure Cooked Jamaican Jerk Pork Roast

Yield: 6 | Total Time: 55 Mins | Prep Time: 10 Mins | Cook Time: 45 Mins

Ingredients

- 2-pound pork shoulder
- 1 tbsp. extra-virgin olive oil
- 1/4 cup Jamaican Jerk spice blend
- 1/2 cup beef stock

Directions

1. Thoroughly rub pork roast with oil and coat with spice blend. Brown the meat in your instant pot under sauté mode and then add in beef broth. Lock lid and cook on manual for 45 Mins and then release pressure naturally. Serve.

Nutrition : Calories: 452; Total Fat: 33.5 g; Carbs: 0 g; Dietary Fiber: 0 g; Sugars: 0 g; Protein: 35.3 g; Cholesterol: 136 mg; Sodium: 135 mg

Instant Pot Crisp Chinese pork with Yummy Broccoli Mash

Yield: 4 | Total Time: 50 Mins | Prep Time: 10 Mins | Cook Time: 40 Mins

Ingredients

- 1-pound piece boned pork
- 3 tablespoons olive oil
- 2 tsp. Chinese five-spice powder

For dipping sauce

- 1 spring onion, finely chopped
- 1 tbsp. Thai sweet chilli sauce
- 1 tbsp. minced ginger
- 4 tbsp. soy sauce

Yummy Broccoli Mash

- 600g fresh/ frozen broccoli
- 4 tablespoons butter
- 1 tsp sea salt
- Freshly ground pepper to taste
- 1/4 cup full fat extra virgin coconut milk

Directions

1. Make the Broccoli Mash: Pour about an inch of water in a medium pot and bring it to a boil, add a steamer basket or colander and steam the broccoli for 5 Mins. Drain and pulse the broccoli in a food processor or blender. Add in butter, salt, pepper and coconut milk and continue pulsing to make a mash.
2. Rub pork with two teaspoons salt and 5-spice and chill, uncovered, in the fridge for at least 2 hours.
3. When ready, add water to your instant pot and insert a metal trivet. Drizzle pork with olive oil and season with salt and pepper; place over the trivet and lock lid. Cook on high for 40 Mins and let pressure come down on its own. Remove from the pot and place it over a chopping board and let it rest for at least 10 Mins before serving.
4. Mix all dipping ingredients and stir in two tablespoons of water. Serve pork with sauce and broccoli mash. Enjoy!

Nutrition : Calories: 406; Fat: 28.3g; Carbs: 10.6g; Protein: 30.3g

Instant Pot Pork Salad

Yield: 4 | Total Time: 40 Mins | Prep Time: 10 Mins | Cook Time: 30 Mins

Ingredients

For the salads
- Salad greens
- 2 plum tomatoes, sliced
- 1 pound pork
- 3 tablespoons olive oil
- ½ cup chopped nuts

Dressing
- 2/3 cup buttermilk
- half of an avocado
- 8-10 chives
- 1 clove of garlic, chopped
- 4 fresh basil leaves
- 1 teaspoon dried minced red onion
- A sprig fresh rosemary
- 1/2 teaspoon dried dill
- A few leaves of fresh parsley
- 1/2 liquid Stevia
- pinch of chicory powder
- 1/4 teaspoon sea salt
- Pinch of pepper

Directions

1. Drizzle pork with olive oil and season with salt and pepper. Add water to an instant pot and insert a trivet; place pork over the trivet and lock lid. Cook on high for 30 Mins and then let pressure come down on its own. Transfer the pork to the oven and cook at 350 degrees for 10 Mins or until crispy.
2. Slice the pork to serve.
3. Mix salad ingredients and divide among serving plates; top each with steak slices, tomato, and mango.
4. In a food processor or blender, blend together dressing ingredients until very smooth; pour over salad and toss to coat well. Enjoy!

Nutrition : Calories: 493; Fat: 35.1g; Carbs: 14.5g; Protein: 37.8g

Instant Pot Citrus Pork

Yield: 4 | Total Time: 1 Hour 25 Mins | Prep Time: 10 Mins | Cook Time: 1 Hour 15 Mins

Ingredients
- 2 pounds pork
- 1 red onion, minced
- Juice of ½ lemon
- Pinch of lemon zest
- Pinch of saffron
- Pinch of ground coriander
- Pinch of ginger
- Pinch of salt & pepper

Directions:

1. Soak saffron in fresh lemon juice; crush into paste and then add dry spices.
2. Dip in pork and rub remaining spices into pork; sprinkle with salt and pepper and wrap in foil.
3. Heat oil in the instant pot on manual high and cook pork for 5 Mins per side or until browned. Remove and transfer to foil. Wrap and set aside.
4. Add water to an instant pot and insert a trivet; place the pork over the trivet and lock lid and cook on manual high for 1 hour.

Nutrition : Calories: 122; Total Fat: 2.6 g; Carbs: 1.9 g; Dietary Fiber: 0.5 g; Sugars: 0.6 g; Protein: 21.4 g; Cholesterol: 64 mg; Sodium: 52 mg

Instant Pot BBQ Pork Ribs

Yield: 5 | Total Time: 2 Hours | Prep Time: 30 Mins | Cook Time: 1 Hour 30 Mins

Ingredients

- 4 tablespoons olive oil
- 2 ½ pounds pork ribs
- 1 cup barbeque sauce
- 1 tablespoon garlic powder
- 2 tablespoons sea salt
- 1 teaspoon ground black pepper
- 5 cups steamed broccoli

Directions

1. Add oil to an instant pot and set on sauté mode, but not smoking. Add in the pork ribs and cook until seared on both sides. Add in enough water to cover the pork ribs and season with salt, garlic powder and pepper. Lock lid and cook on meat/stew for 20 Mins and the quick release the pressure.
2. Preheat your oven to 325 degrees.
3. Transfer the ribs to a baking dish and pour over the barbecue sauce. Cover with foil and bake for about 1 hour 30 Mins. Remove and let rest for at least 10 Mins before serving. Serve with steamed broccoli. Enjoy!

Nutrition : Calories: 556; Fat: 37.9g; Carbs: 6.4g; Protein: 46.3g

Instant Pot Spiced Pork Chops

Yield: 4 | Prep Time: 5 Mins | Cook Time: 10 Mins | Total Time: 15 Mins

Ingredients

Pork Chops

- 4 (100g each) boneless pork chops
- ½ tsp garlic paste
- 1 tsp lemon juice
- 1 tbsp. Worcestershire sauce
- 4 tbsp. olive oil
- ½ tsp ground cumin
- ½ tsp onion powder
- 1 tsp paprika
- A pinch of salt
- A pinch of pepper

Steamed Veggies

- 1 head broccoli, cut into florets
- 1 head cauliflower, cut into florets
- 2 zucchinis, halved and sliced
- 5 ginger-lemongrass tea bags
- A two-inch ginger root, chopped roughly
- Freshly ground pepper to taste

Directions

1. **Prepare the Veggies:** Add the water to the bottom of an instant pot and add the chopped ginger. Add the tea bags once the water boils together with the pepper and a pinch of salt. Let the tea steep for 5 Mins. Add the steamer basket or colander start by placing the broccoli and cauliflower at the bottom. Season with salt and pepper and top with zucchini. Lock lid and cook on high for 5 Mins and then quick release the pressure.
2. **For the Pork Chops:** Combine all ingredients in a bag; add in the pork chops and massage the marinade around the meat. Remove the meat from the marinade and discard the marinade; season the meat with salt and pepper. Cook the pork in the pot on manual high 5 Mins per side or until cooked through.
3. Serve the pork chops with the steamed veggies. Enjoy!

Nutrition : Calories: 275; Fat: 17.3g; Carbs: 5.9g; Protein: 24.1g

Instant Pot Pork Chops

Yield: 2 | Total Time: 15 Mins | Prep Time: 5 Mins | Cook Time: 10 Mins

Ingredients

- 2 boneless pork chops
- 4 slices tomato
- 2 slices of fresh mozzarella
- 1 tbsp. olive oil
- 1 tbsp. butter
- A pinch of sea salt
- A pinch of pepper
- 2 cups green salad to serve

Directions

1. Rub the pork chops with salt and pepper; melt butter and olive oil in an instant pot. Add the pork chops and sear for about 3 Mins per side.
2. Transfer the pork chops to a baking sheet and place tomato slices and mozzarella cheese on top. Broil the meat on high for 5 Mins or until cheese is melted. Serve with a green salad.

Nutrition : Calories: 421; Fat: 33g; Carbs: 2.4g; Protein: 32

Lemon & Herb Pork Chops

Yield: 4 | Total Time: 35 Mins | Prep Time: 5 Mins | Cook Time: 30 Mins

Ingredients

- 4 large bone in thick pork chops
- 1 tbsp. Italian seasoning
- 1/3 cup lemon juice
- 1 tbsp. minced garlic
- 3 tbsp. extra virgin olive oil
- 1 teaspoon salt

Steamed Spring Veggies

- 3 small zucchinis, quartered lengthways
- 1 bunch asparagus, woody ends removed
- 1 bunch baby carrots, trimmed
- 1 tbsp. white balsamic vinegar
- 2 tsp. fresh lemon zest
- 40g butter

Directions

1. **Prepare the Veggies:** Place the baby carrots in a steamer set over a saucepan of boiling water; cover and cook for about 5 Mins. Add zucchini and asparagus and cook, covered, for 2 Mins more or until the veggies are tender crisp. In a large frying pan, heat butter until melted and foamy; add the lemon zest and cook for about 30 seconds. Stir in the steamed veggies and vinegar; toss until well coated. Season with salt and pepper and serve.
2. **For the Pork Chops:** In a small bowl, whisk together olive oil, lemon juice, Italian seasoning, garlic and salt until well combined. In a plastic bag, combine the pork chops and marinade; seal and shake to coat the chops well and then refrigerate overnight. When ready, set your instant pot on manual high and add in oil. Cook the pork chops for 10 Mins per side and remove from the pot. Add water to the pot and insert a trivet. Place the chops on the trivet and cook on meat setting for 10 Mins. Let pressure come down on its own.

Nutrition : Calories: 517; Fat: 35.7g; Carbs: 6g; Protein: 41.6

Instant Pot Pork Rind Stuffed Peppers

Yield: 4 | Total Time: 30 Mins | Prep Time: 10 Mins | Cook Time: 20 Mins

Ingredients

- 1 tablespoon butter
- 3 Green/red/yellow peppers, top parts cut off
- 1/2 cup celery, chopped
- 2 tablespoons onion, chopped
- 5 ounces pork rinds, crushed
- 2 eggs
- 2 ounces chicken broth
- 2 tablespoons heavy cream
- Pepper
- 1 teaspoon granular Splenda
- Poultry seasoning

Directions

1. Melt butter in a skillet and sauté onion, celery and seasonings until onion is tender. Transfer to a bowl and mix in all ingredients, except the peppers. Stuff the mixture into each pepper and arrange them on a foil. Add water to an instant pot and insert a metal trivet; place the peppers over the trivet and lock lid. Cook on high for 20 Mins and then let pressure come down on its own.

Nutrition : Calories: 572; Total Fat: 45.1 g; Carbs: 17.2 g; Dietary Fiber: 1.6 g; Sugars: 4.4 g Protein: 29.9 g; Cholesterol: 220 mg; Sodium: 276 mg

Keto Instant Spiced Pork Chops

Yield: 4 | Total Time: 2 Hours 10 Mins | Prep Time: 10 Mins | Cook Time: 2 Hours

Ingredients

- 2 pounds pork chops
- 4 tbsp. olive oil
- 1 tbsp. fennel seeds
- 1 tbsp. chives chopped, fresh
- 1 tbsp. curry powder dried
- 1 tbsp. thyme dried
- 1 tbsp. rosemary dried
- 1 tbsp. ground cumin
- 1 tsp salt
- 4 cups chopped cauliflower, steamed

Directions

1. In a bowl, mix together fennel seeds, chives, curry powder, thyme, rosemary, half of olive oil, cumin and salt until well combined; rub the pork chops with the oil-spice mixture until well coated.
2. Heat the remaining oil in the instant pot and add in pork meat. Cover and cook on high for at least 2 hours. Serve the pork chops with steamed cauliflower.

Nutrition : Calories: 257; Fat: 15.1g; Carbs: 1.2g; Protein: 24.1g

Instant Pot Cheese Crusted Pork Chops

Yield: 4 | Total Time: 46 Mins | Prep Time: 6 Mins | Cook Time: 40 Mins

Ingredients

- 4 (1 ¼ pound) boneless pork chops
- 2 tbsp. olive oil
- ½ teaspoon sea salt
- ½ teaspoon pepper
- 2 tsp water
- 1 large egg, beaten
- 1/2 cup crushed pork rinds
- 1/2 tsp lemon zest
- 1/2 cup grated parmesan cheese
- 1/2 tsp minced fresh garlic
- 1 tbsp. minced fresh parsley
- 4 cups spinach
- 1 tablespoon butter
- 2 red onions, chopped

Directions

1. Using a paper towel, pat pork dry and then season with salt and pepper.
2. In a shallow bowl, whisk together the egg and water until well combined.
3. In a bowl, mix together parmesan cheese with crushed pork rinds, parsley, lemon zest, minced garlic until well combined.
4. Add oil to an instant pot and set on sauté mode; dip the pork chops into the egg mix and then coat well with the cheese mixture. Place the coated pork chops in the pot and cook for about 3 Mins; flip over to cook the other side for 3 Mins more or until cooked through and crispy on the outside. Transfer the cooked chops to foil and wrap well. Add water to the pot and insert a trivet. Place the pork on the trivet and lock lid. Set your pot on meat/stew setting for 20 Mins. Quick release the pressure and remove the pork. Let rest for about 10 Mins before serving.
5. Heat butter in a skillet over medium heat; sauté red onions until fragrant. Stir in spinach for about 3 Mins or until wilted; season with salt and pepper and serve with pork chops.

Nutrition : Calories: 493; Fat: 35.1g; Carbs: 14.5g; Protein: 37.8g

Pork Chops in Cream Sauce served with Avocado

Yield: 6 | Total Time: 25 Mins | Prep Time: 10 Mins | Cook Time: 15 Mins

Ingredients

- 2 lb. boneless pork chops
- 4 tablespoons butter
- 4 cups sliced fresh mushrooms
- 2 cups heavy cream
- 3/4 cup white wine
- A pinch of sea salt
- A pinch of pepper
- 4 avocados, diced

Directions

1. Set your instant pot on manual high and melt in butter. Season the pork chops with sea salt and pepper; arrange the chops in the pot and fry for about 2 Mins per side or until browned. Stir in wine and cook for 6 Mins; remove the pork chops from the pot and place on a plate. Stir the cream in the pot and stir in mushrooms and pork chops and lock lid. Cook on high for 6 Mins and press venting button to release the pressure. Serve hot topped with Avocado slices. Enjoy!

Nutrition : Calories: 540; Fat: 37.3g; Carbs: 10.8g; Protein: 42g

Caramelized Onion Pork Chops with Steamed Green Beans and Avocado

Yield: 6 | Total Time: 45 Mins | Prep Time: 5 Mins | Cook Time: 40 Mins

Ingredients

- 4 tablespoon vegetable oil
- 2 cups sliced onions
- 2 lb. pork loin chops
- 3 teaspoons seasoning salt
- 2 teaspoons ground black pepper
- 1 onion, cut into strips
- 1 cup water
- 2 cups chopped green beans, steamed
- 3 avocados, diced

Directions

1. Season the chops with salt and pepper; heat oil in an instant pot set on manual high and brown the chops for about 5 Mins per side. Stir in onions and water and lock lid. Cook on high for 20 Mins and then quick release the pressure.
2. Meanwhile, add the remaining oil to a skillet set over medium-low heat; add in onions and cook, stirring, for about 10 Mins or until caramelized.
3. Serve the chops with caramelized onions and steamed green beans topped with avocado slices. Enjoy!

Nutrition : Calories: 595; Fat: 41g; Carbs: 16.8g; Protein: 42.1g

INSTANT POT KETO SEAFOOD AND FISH RECIPES

Instant Pot Coconut Fishbowl

Yield: 8 | Total Time: 20 Mins | Prep Time: 5 Mins | Cook Time: 15 Mins

Ingredients

- 1 ½ pounds fish fillets, sliced into bite-size pieces
- 2 cups coconut milk
- 1 tbsp. freshly grated ginger
- 2 garlic cloves, minced
- 2 medium onions, chopped
- 2 green chilies, sliced into strips
- 1 tomato, chopped
- 6 curry leaves
- 3 tbsp. curry powder mix
- 2 tbsp. fresh lemon juice
- 2 tsp. salt

Directions

1. Set your instant pot on sauté mode and add oil; sauté curry leaves for 1 minute and then add ginger, garlic and onion; cook until tender; stir in curry powder mix and cook for 2 Mins or until fragrant.
2. Add coconut milk and then stir in fish, tomatoes, and green chilies until well combined; lock lid and cook on high for 5 Mins. Let pressure come down naturally and then stir in lemon juice and salt.

Nutrition : Calories: 296; Total Fat: 11.1 g; Carbs: 13.4g; Dietary Fiber: 0.2 g; sugars: 6.5g; Protein: 26.8 g; Cholesterol: 88 mg; Sodium: 1121 mg

Instant Pot Shrimp Paella

Yield: 4 | Total Time: 20 Mins | Prep Time: 10 Mins | Cook Time: 10 Mins

Ingredients

- 1-pound jumbo shrimp
- 4 tbsp. butter
- 1 red pepper chopped
- 4 cloves garlic chopped
- 1 onion chopped
- 1/2 cup white wine
- 1 cup chicken broth
- 1/4 cup cilantro
- 1/4 tsp red pepper flakes
- 1 pinch saffron threads
- 1 tsp turmeric
- 1 tsp paprika
- 1/2 tsp salt
- 1/4 tsp black pepper

Directions

1. Set your instant pot on sauté mode and melt in butter; stir in onion until tender and then add in garlic; cook for 1 minute and then stir in spices. Cook for 1 minute and then add red peppers. Stir in wine and chicken broth. Add in shrimp and lock lid; cook on manual for 5 Mins. Let pressure come down naturally; stir in cilantro and serve.

Nutrition : Calories: 314; Total Fat: 17.1 g; Carbs: 10.1g; Dietary Fiber: 0.1 g; sugars: 0.4g; Protein: 31.1 g; Cholesterol: 91 mg; Sodium: 698 mg

Steamed Alaskan Crab Legs

Yield: 6 | Total Time: 10 Mins | Prep Time: 5 Mins | Cook Time: 5 Mins

Ingredients

- 3 pounds crab legs
- 1 cup water
- 1/2 tbsp. salt
- melted butter

Directions

1. Place a steamer basket in your instant pot and add a cup of water and salt to the pot; add crab legs to the basket and lock lid; cook on manual high for 5 Mins. Quick release pressure and then serve the steamed crab legs with melted butter.

Nutrition : Calories: 246; Total Fat: 5.4 g; Carbs: 0g; Dietary Fiber: 0 g; sugars: 0g; Protein: 43.6 g; Cholesterol: 131 mg; Sodium: 3026 mg

Instant Pot Shrimp & Grits

Yield: 4 | Total Time: 40 Mins | Prep Time: 15 Mins | Cook Time: 25 Mins

Ingredients

Shrimp Ingredients

- 3 strips smoked bacon, diced
- 1-pound shrimp, peeled and deveined
- 1 tbsp. garlic, minced
- 1/2 cup bell peppers, chopped
- 1/3 cup onion, chopped
- 1 1/2 cups diced tomatoes
- 2 tsp. Old Bay seasoning
- 1/4 tsp hot sauce
- 2 tbsp. lemon juice
- 1/4 cup chicken broth
- 2 tbsp. dry white wine
- 1/2 tsp salt
- 1/4 tsp pepper
- 1/4 cup heavy cream
- 1/4 cup scallions, sliced

Grits Ingredients

- 1/2 cup grits
- 1 tbsp. butter
- 1 cup milk
- salt & pepper
- 1 cup water

Directions

1. Season shrimp with Old Bay seasoning and set aside.
2. Set your instant pot on sauté mode and cook bacon for 3 Mins or until crisp; transfer to a plate. Add bell peppers and onions to the pot and cook for about 3 Mins; stir in garlic and cook for 1 minute.
3. Turn off your pot and then stir in white wine to deglaze; stir in hot sauce, broth, lemon juice, tomatoes, salt and pepper and then add in a trivet.
4. In a heat-proof bowl, mix together milk, grits, salt, water and pepper and place it over the trivet; lock lid and cook on manual for 10 Mins; let pressure come down on its own. Remove the grits and trivet and the stir in shrimp; lock lid and let shrimp cook. Fluff grits and add butter. Stir the shrimp and then turn the pot on sauté mode; stir in cream and serve with grits garnished with bacon and scallions.

Nutrition : Calories: 385; Total Fat: 19.4 g; Carbs: 13.9g; Dietary Fiber: 2.9 g; sugars: 9.6g; Protein: 38.6 g; Cholesterol: 201 mg; Sodium: 873 mg

Salmon with Gingery Orange Sauce

Yield: 4 | Total Time: 15 Mins | Prep Time: 10 Mins | Cook Time: 5 Mins

Ingredients

- 1-pound salmon
- 1 tbsp. dark soy sauce
- 2 tbsp. marmalade
- 1 tsp. minced garlic
- 2 tsp. minced ginger
- 1 tsp. salt
- 1 ½ tsp pepper

Directions

1. Add fish to a Ziplock bag; mix all remaining ingredients and add to the bag; let marinate for at least 15 Mins.
2. Add two cups of water to your instant pot and add in a steamer rack. Place the bag with fish on the rack and lock lid; cook on high for 5 Mins and then let pressure come down on its own.

Nutrition : Calories: 281; Total Fat: 7.9g; Carbs: 10.1g; Dietary Fiber: 0.4 g; sugars: 7.1g; Protein: 22.2 g; Cholesterol: 50 mg; Sodium: 653 mg

Instant Pot Mussels

Yield: 4 | Total Time: 25 Mins | Prep Time: 15 Mins | Cook Time: 10 Mins

Ingredients

- 2 pounds mussels, cleaned
- 2 tbsp. butter
- 4 garlic cloves, minced
- 2 shallots, chopped
- 1/2 cup white wine
- 1/2 cup broth
- 1 tbsp. fresh lemon juice
- 1 tbsp. chopped parsley

Directions

1. Melt butter in your instant pot under sauté mode and cook onion until tender; stir in garlic and cook for 1 minute; stir in wine and broth and then turn off the pot.
2. Add the mussels and lock lid; cook on manual for 5 Mins and then release pressure naturally.
3. Serve with fresh lemon juice and parsley.

Nutrition : Calories: 285; Total Fat: 11.1 g; Carbs: 11.3g; Dietary Fiber: 0.1 g; sugars: 0.4g; Protein: 28.1 g; Cholesterol: 79 mg; Sodium: 789 mg

Salmon w/ Chili-Lime Sauce

Yield: 2 | Total Time: 15 Mins | Prep Time: 10 Mins | Cook Time: 5 Mins

Ingredients

For steaming salmon:
- 2 salmon fillets
- 1 cup water

- sea salt & pepper

For chili-lime sauce:
- 1 jalapeno seeds removed and diced
- 2 cloves garlic minced
- 2 tbsp. lime juice
- 1 tbsp. olive oil

- 1 tbsp. chopped parsley
- 1/2 tsp. cumin
- 1/2 tsp. paprika
- 1 tbsp. liquid Stevia
- 1 tbsp. hot water

Directions

1. In a bowl, mix all sauce ingredients and set aside.
2. Add water to your instant pot and place salmon in a steamer basket inside the pot; sprinkle fish with salt and pepper and then lock lid; cook on high for 5 Mins and then let pressure come down naturally.
3. Transfer fish to a plate and drizzle with sauce to serve.

Nutrition : Calories: 319; Total Fat: 21.2 g; Carbs: 10.8g; Dietary Fiber: 3.4 g; sugars: 6.7g; Protein: 22.8 g; Cholesterol: 13 mg; Sodium: 715 mg

Instant Pot Tilapia

Yield: 6 | Total Time: 2 Hours 15 Mins | Prep Time: 15 Mins | Cook Time: 15 Mins

Ingredients

- 6 tilapia filets
- 1 bundle of asparagus
- 12 tbsp. lemon juice

- Lemon pepper seasoning
- 3 tbsp. melted coconut oil

Directions

1. Divide asparagus into equal amounts per each fillet.
2. Place each fillet in the center of a piece of foil and sprinkle with about 1 tsp. lemon pepper seasoning; drizzle with about 2 tbsp. lemon juice and about ½ tbsp. melted coconut oil. Top each filet with the asparagus and fold the foil to form a packet. Repeat with the remaining ingredients and then place the packets into an instant pot. Lock lid and cook on high for 15 Mins.

Nutrition : Calories: 181; Total Fat: 11.5 g; Carbs: 1.8 g; Dietary Fiber: 0.7 g; Sugars: 1.3 g; Protein: 27.3 g; Cholesterol: 60 mg; Sodium: 404 mg

Pressure Cooked Coconut Curry Shrimp

Yield: 4 | Total Time: 15 Mins | Prep Time: 5 Mins | Cook Time: 10 Mins

Ingredients

- 1 pound shelled shrimp
- 15 ounces water
- 4 cups coconut milk
- ½ cup Thai red curry sauce
- ¼ cup cilantro
- 2½ tsp. garlic-lemon seasoning

Directions

1. In your instant pot, combine water, coconut milk, red curry paste, cilantro, and lemon garlic seasoning; stir to mix well and lock lid; cook on high for 10 Mins and then release the pressure quickly. Add shrimp and continue cooking for another five Mins and then release pressure naturally.
2. Serve garnished with cilantro.

Nutrition : Calories: 624; Total Fat: 52.6 g; Carbs: 13.5 g; Dietary Fiber: 4.7 g; Sugars: 7.1 g; Protein: 30.7 g; Cholesterol: 239 mg; Sodium: 312 mg

Hot Lemony Tilapia w/ Asparagus

Yield: 6 | Total Time: 30 Mins | Prep Time: 15 Mins | Cook Time: 15 Mins

Ingredients

- 6 tilapia filets
- 1 bundle of asparagus
- 12 tbsp. lemon juice
- Lemon pepper seasoning
- 3 tbsp. melted coconut oil

Directions

1. Divide asparagus into equal amounts per each fillet.
2. Place each fillet in the center of a piece of foil and sprinkle with about 1 tsp. lemon pepper seasoning; drizzle with about 2 tbsp. lemon juice and about ½ tbsp. melted coconut oil. Top each filet with the asparagus and fold the foil to form a packet. Repeat with the remaining ingredients and then place the packets into an instant pot. Lock lid and cook on high for 15 Mins.

Nutrition : Calories: 181; Total Fat: 11.5 g; Carbs: 1.8 g; Dietary Fiber: 0.7 g; Sugars: 1.3 g; Protein: 27.3 g; Cholesterol: 60 mg; Sodium: 404 mg

Tasty Citrus Tilapia

Yield: 4 | Total Time: 25 Mins | Prep Time: 10 Mins | Cook Time: 15 Mins

Ingredients

- 4 tilapia filets
- 1-10-ounce can mandarin oranges
- 2 tbsp. minced garlic
- 3 tbsp. coconut oil
- Sea salt and pepper

Directions

1. Arrange fish side by side on a large piece of aluminum foil and sprinkle with garlic and coconut oil evenly. Top the fish with oranges and season with salt and pepper; fold the foil to wrap the contents well.
2. Place in an instant pot and lock lid; cook on high for 15 Mins.

Nutrition : Calories: 201; Total Fat: 19.3 g; Carbs: 8.2 g; Dietary Fiber: 0.6 g; Sugars: 6.3 g; Protein: 22.7 g; Cholesterol: 50 mg; Sodium: 334 mg

Pressure Steamed Salmon

Yield: 4 | Total Time: 21 Mins | Prep Time: 15 Mins | Cook Time: 6 Mins

Ingredients

- 1 tablespoon extra-virgin olive oil
- 6 ounces wild salmon fillets, skinless
- Fennel fronds
- 1 tablespoon chopped parsley
- 1 tablespoon chopped dill
- 1 tablespoon chopped chives
- 1 tablespoon chopped tarragon
- 1 tablespoon chopped basil
- 1 tablespoon chopped shallot
- 1 tablespoon lemon juice

Directions

1. Add water to an instant pot and insert a trivet; place salmon and fennel wedges over the trivet and lock lid. Cook on high for 6 Mins. In a bowl, combine the chopped herbs, extra virgin olive oil, and shallot and lemon juice; stir until well combined. Season and spoon over cooked fish.

Nutrition : Calories: 98; Total Fat: 6.3 g; Carbs: 2.5 g; Dietary Fiber: 0.9 g; sugars: trace; Protein: 8.9 g; Cholesterol: 19 mg; Sodium: 33 mg

Teriyaki Fish w/ Zucchini

Yields: 2 | Total Time: 40 Mins | Prep Time: 10 Mins | Cook Time: 30 Mins

Ingredients

- 2 (6-ounce) salmon fillets
- 7 tablespoons teriyaki sauce (low sodium)
- 2 tablespoons sesame seeds
- 2 teaspoons canola oil
- 4 scallions, chopped
- 2 small zucchinis, thinly sliced

Directions

1. Mix fish with 5 tablespoons of teriyaki sauce in a zip-top bag and marinate for at least 20 Mins.
2. Set your instant pot on manual high, toast sesame seeds; set aside. Drain the marinated fish and discard the marinade.
3. Add fish to the pot and cook for about 5 Mins per side; remove fish from skillet and keep warm.
4. Add oil, scallions and zucchini to the skillet and sauté for about 4 Mins or until browned.
5. Stir in the remaining teriyaki sauce and lock lid. Cook on high for 5 Mins and then let pressure come down. Sprinkle with toasted sesame seeds and serve with fish.

Nutrition : Calories: 408; Total Fat: 19.9 g; Carbs: 8.1 g; Dietary Fiber: 4.3 g; Protein: 40.3 g; Cholesterol: 75 mg; Sodium: 2505 mg; sugars: 11.7 g

Grilled Tuna w/ Bean & Tomato Salad

Yields: 4 | Total Time: 23 Mins | Prep Time: 10 Mins | Cook Time: 13 Mins

Ingredients

- 1 ½ tablespoons extra virgin olive oil
- 3 scallions, thinly sliced
- 1 tablespoon fresh lemon juice
- 1/4 cup fresh tarragon leaves
- 1 (15 ounces) can beans, drained, rinsed
- 1 pound heirloom tomatoes, cored, diced
- Sea salt
- 4 (8 ounce) tuna steaks

Directions

1. In a bowl, mix together oil, scallions, lemon juice, tarragon, beans, tomatoes, and salt; set aside.
2. Set your instant pot on manual high and heat in oil; add in tuna and cook for 4 Mins per side. Add in coconut milk and cook on high for 5 Mins. Let pressure come down. Serve tuna with bean salad.

Nutrition : Calories: 505; Total Fat: 19.8g; Carbs: 9.4g; Dietary Fiber: 4g; Protein: 70.4g; Cholesterol: 111mg; Sodium: 123mg; sugars: 1.8g

Steamed Bass with Fennel, Parsley, and Capers

Yields: 2 | Total Time: 30 Mins | Prep Time: 15 Mins | Cook Time: 15 Mins

Ingredients

- 2- 5-ounce portions of striped bass
- 2 tablespoons extra-virgin olive oil
- 1/2 lemon, juiced
- 1 fennel bulb, sliced
- 1/4 medium onion, sliced
- 1/4 cup chopped parsley
- 1 tablespoon capers, rinsed
- 1/2 teaspoon sea salt
- Chopped parsley and olive oil, for garnish

Directions

1. Add lemon juice, fennel and onion to an instant pot and cover with 1-inch water; bring the mixture to a gentle boil on manual high. Add seasoned fish and sprinkle with parsley and capers; lock lid and cook on high for 10 Mins. Let pressure come down on its own.
2. Transfer to a serving bowl and drizzle with extra virgin olive oil and top with more parsley to serve.

Nutrition : Calories: 325; Total Fat: 24.6g; Carbs: 10.5g; Dietary Fiber: 4.3g; Protein: 10.9g; Cholesterol: 0mg; Sodium: 661mg; sugars: 0.7g

Pressure Baked Salmon Salad with Mint Dressing

Yield: 1 Serving | Total Time: 30 Mins | Prep Time: 10 Mins | Cook Time: 20 Mins

Ingredients

- 130g salmon fillet
- 1 tablespoon olive oil
- 2 red onions, thinly sliced
- 1 cucumber (50g) cucumber, sliced
- 2 radishes, thinly sliced
- ¼ cup baby spinach
- ½ cup mixed salad leaves
- ½ cup chopped parsley

The dressing:

- 1 tbsp. rice vinegar
- 1 tablespoon olive oil
- 1 tbsp. natural yogurt
- 1 tsp. mayonnaise
- 1 tbsp. finely chopped mint leaves
- salt and black pepper

Directions

1. Set your instant pot to manual high and heat olive oil; add in fish and cook for 3 Mins per side; remove the fish to a plate. Add water to the pot and insert a trivet; place the fish over the trivet and lock lid. Cook on high for 10 Mins and then naturally release the pressure.
2. In a bowl, mix together rice wine vinegar, yogurt, oil, mayonnaise, mint, salt and pepper; let stand for at least 5 Mins for flavors to blend.
3. Arrange salad leaves and spinach on a plate and top with red onions, cucumber, radishes, and parsley. Flake the fish and place onto the salad; drizzle with the mint dressing and serve.

Nutrition : Calories: 258; Total Fat: 21.4g; Carbs: 13.5g; Dietary Fiber: 4.3g; Protein: 31g;

Spiced Mahi-Mahi with Creamed Sautéed Mushrooms

Yield: 2 | Total Time: 35 Mins | Prep Time: 15 Mins | Cook Time: 20 Mins

Ingredients

- 1 ¾ tsps. ground cumin
- 1/2 tsp. garlic powder
- 1/2 tsp. dried oregano
- 1/4 tsp. ground ginger
- 1/4 tsp. smoked paprika
- 1/4 tsp. kosher salt
- 1/4 tsp. ground black pepper
- 1/8 tsp. ground red pepper
- 1 tbsp. olive oil
- 2 Mahi Mahi fillets
- Grilling Spray
- 1 cup cream cheese
- 4 cups button mushrooms
- 2 tablespoons butter
- 1 red onion, chopped

Directions

1. Mix ¾ tsp. cumin, garlic powder, dried oregano, ground ginger, smoked paprika, salt and red and black pepper in a small bowl. Add in olive oil to make a spicy paste; divide mixture in half and set one portion aside.
2. Rub half of the spice mix on the fish fillets then put aside. Set your instant pot to manual high and then add the fish; cook for 3-4 Mins per side, turning once.
3. Remove grilled fish as soon as it easily flakes when pierced with a fork. Brush the remaining fish with the remaining spice rub.
4. Add butter to the pot and sauté red onion until fragrant; stir in mushrooms, whipping cream, salt and pepper. Lock lid and cook for 5 Mins on high. Let pressure come down naturally. Serve the fish over the creamed mushrooms.

Nutrition : Calories: 157; Total Fat: 7g; Carbs: 4g; Protein: 20g;

Instant Pot Seafood Cioppino

Yield: 2 | Total Time: 50 Mins | Prep Time: 10 Mins | Cook Time: 40 Mins

Ingredients

- 3 ounces lump crabmeat
- 3 ounces chopped clams
- 3 ounces shrimp, peeled, deveined
- 3 ounces haddock fillets, sliced
- 1 tbsp. olive oil
- 3 celery ribs, chopped
- ¼ cup chopped onions
- 2 garlic cloves, minced
- 1 cup canned tomatoes
- 4 tbsp. tomato paste
- ½ cup clam juice
- 1 tbsp. red wine vinegar
- 1/2 cup vegetable broth
- 2 tsp. Italian seasoning
- 2 tbsp. minced fresh parsley
- 1/2 tsp. sugar
- 1 bay leaf

Directions

1. In an instant pot, combine all ingredients except seafood and parsley. Cook for 10 Mins and then stir in seafood. Cook on high for about 30 Mins. Let pressure come down and then discard bay leaf and stir in parsley. Serve.

Nutrition : Calories: 339; Total Fat: 19.3 g; Carbs: 13.8g; Dietary Fiber: 3.3 g; sugars: 8.8g; Protein: 22.8 g; Cholesterol: 107 mg; Sodium: 1124 mg

Instant Pot Shrimp Scampi

Yield: 2 | Total Time: 1 Hours 10 Mins | Prep Time: 10 Mins | Cook Time: 1 Hour

Ingredients

- ½ pound shrimp, peeled, deveined
- 2 tbsp. butter
- 2 tbsp. olive oil
- 1 tbsp. minced garlic
- 1/4 cup chicken broth
- 2 tbsp. parsley
- 1/2 squeezed lemon
- salt & pepper

Directions

1. Combine all ingredients in your instant pot; lock lid and cook on high for about 1 hour. Let pressure come down on its own. Serve over steamed veggies.

Nutrition : Calories: 223; Total Fat: 17.8 g; Carbs: 5.3g; Dietary Fiber: 0.3 g; sugars: 4.8g; Protein: 24.8 g; Cholesterol: 106 mg; Sodium: 917 mg

Instant Pot BBQ Shrimp

Yield: 2 | Total Time: 40 Mins | Prep Time: 10 Mins | Cook Time: 30 Mins

Ingredients

- 2 tbsp. butter
- ½ pound peeled, deveined shrimp
- 2 tsp minced garlic
- 1/4 cup BBQ sauce
- 2 tbsp. Worcestershire sauce
- Salt & pepper
- Lemon wedges,

Directions

1. Add shrimp to your instant pot and add the remaining ingredients except lemon wedge; lock lid and cook on high for 30 Mins. Naturally release the pressure. Serve warm, garnished with lemon wedge and a side dish of veggies.

Nutrition : Calories: 247; Total Fat: 7.8 g; Carbs: 13.7g; Dietary Fiber: 0.3 g; sugars: 9.7g; Protein: 26 g; Cholesterol: 254 mg; Sodium: 750 mg

Spicy Grilled Cod

Yields: 4 | Total Time: 35 Mins | Prep Time: 15 Mins | Cook Time: 20 Mins

Ingredients

- 1-pound cod filets
- 2 tablespoons extra virgin olive oil
- 2 minced garlic cloves
- 1/8 teaspoon cayenne pepper
- 3 tablespoons fresh lime juice
- 1 ½ teaspoon fresh lemon juice
- ¼ cup freshly squeezed orange juice
- 1/3 cup water
- 1 tablespoon chopped fresh thyme
- 2 tablespoon chopped fresh chives

Healthy Steamed Vegetables

- 1 head broccoli
- 2 red bell peppers, sliced in bite-sized lengths
- 1/4 cup zucchini, sliced into rounds
- 2 baby carrots, sliced into rounds

Direction

1. **Prepare Veggies:** Add water to an instant pot, up to 1 ½ inches from the bottom; set the steamer inside the pot and heat over medium high heat or until the water boils. Add the veggies to the steamer and season with salt and garlic powder. Lock lid and cook for 5 Mins on high setting. Let pressure come down naturally

2. In a bowl, mix together lemon juice, lime juice, orange juice, cayenne pepper, extra virgin olive oil, garlic and water. Place fish in a dish and add the marinade, reserving ¼ cup; marinate in the refrigerator for at least 30 Mins. Broil or grill the marinated fish for about 4 Mins per side, basting regularly with the marinade. Serve the grilled fish on a plate with steamed veggies topped with chives, thyme and the reserved marinade.

Nutritional Information per Serving:

Calories: 200; Total Fat: 8.1 g; Carbs: 5.5 g; Dietary Fiber: 0.5 g; Sugars: 2 g; Protein: 26.4 g; Cholesterol: 62 mg; Sodium: 91 mg

Coconut Fish & Vegetable Curry

Yield: 2 | Total Time: 25 Mins | Prep Time: 5 Mins | Cook Time: 20 Mins

Ingredients

- 300g firm white fish, cubed
- 450g spinach, roughly chopped
- 100g coconut cream
- 2 ½ tbsp. Thai curry paste
- 2 tbsp. coconut oil
- 100ml water
- Kosher salt and pepper, to taste

Directions

1. Add the oil to an instant pot set on manual high. Stir in the curry paste and cook for 3 Mins to bring the spices to life.
2. Pour in the coconut cream and water and bring the sauce to a boil.
3. Add in the fish cubes and lock lid. Cook on high for 15 Mins and then let pressure come down on its own.
4. Gently stir in the spinach and cook for 3 Mins until it wilts.
5. Serve hot!

Nutrition : Calories: 550; Total Fat: 49.5 g; Carbs: 15.9g; Protein: 20.3g

Red Snapper in Hot Veggie Sauce

Yields: 4 | Total Time: 35 Mins | Prep Time: 15 Mins | Cook Time: 20 Mins

Ingredients

- 2-pounds red snapper filets
- ¼ cup canola or extra virgin olive oil
- ½ red bell pepper, chopped
- ½ green bell pepper, chopped
- 4 scallions, thinly sliced
- 2 tomatoes, diced
- 2 cloves garlic
- 2 tablespoon fresh lemon juice
- ½ cup freshly squeezed lime juice
- 1 teaspoon cayenne pepper
- 1 teaspoon pepper
- Cilantro for garnish

Directions

1. Add extra virgin olive oil to an instant pot set on manual high and sauté garlic for about 4 Mins or until golden brown. Place fish in the oil and drizzle with lemon and lime juice. Sprinkle with black pepper and cayenne pepper and top with green and red bell peppers, scallions, and tomatoes.
2. Lock lid and cook on high for 15 Mins and then quick release the pressure.
3. To serve, garnish with cilantro.

Nutrition : Calories: 431; Total Fat: 16.9 g; Carbs: 7 g; Dietary Fiber: 1.9 g; Sugars: 3.7 g; Protein: 61 g; Cholesterol: 107 mg; Sodium: 138 mg

Pressure Grilled Salmon

Yields: 6 | Total Time: 4 Hs 27 Mins | Prep Time: 4 Hs 15 Mins | Cook Time: 12 Mins

Ingredients

- 6 (180 grams each) Atlantic salmon fillets, with skin on
- 1/4 cup extra virgin olive oil
- 1 bunch roughly chopped lemon thyme
- 1/3 cup finely chopped dill leaves
- 2 tablespoons drained and chopped capers
- 2 fresh lemons, juiced
- 2 garlic cloves, finely chopped
- A pinch of sea salt
- Lemon wedges, to garnish

Directions

1. In a large jug, mix together lemon thyme, dill, capers, vinegar, garlic, extra virgin olive oil, sea salt and pepper.
2. Arrange salmon fillets, in a single layer, in a ceramic dish and pour over half of the marinade. Turn it over and pour over the remaining marinade. Refrigerate, covered, for about 4 hours.
3. Remove the fish from the refrigerator at least 30 Mins before cooking.
4. Spray the instant pot with oil and cook the fish, skin side down, for about 3 Mins. Turn and continue barbecuing, basting occasionally with the marinade until browned on both sides. Add a splash of the marinade and lock lid. Cook on high for 6 Mins and then quick release the pressure.
5. Serve garnished with lemon wedges.

Nutrition : Calories: 317; Total Fat: 19.6 g; Carbs: 1.9 g; Dietary Fiber: 0.5 g; Sugars: 0.3 g Protein: 35.3 g; Cholesterol: 79 mg; Sodium: 102 mg

Creamy Coconut Baked Salmon with Green Salad

Yields: 2 | Total Time: 45 Mins | Prep Time: 15 Mins | Cook Time: 20 Mins

Ingredients

For Salmon
- 15-ounce salmon filet
- 1 tablespoon mustard
- A pinch of sea salt
- ½ cup coconut milk
- 2 tablespoons coconut cream

For Salad
- 2 tablespoon dried cranberries
- 2 tablespoon chopped pecans
- 1/2 cup chopped baby spinach
- 1 cup chopped arugula

Directions

1. Preheat your oven to 350°F.
2. Grease a baking sheet with extra virgin olive oil and place on salmon filet; pat dry with paper towels and sprinkle with ground mustard, covering the entire top of fish. Bake for about 15 Mins or until fish flakes easily with a fork.
3. Place the fish in an instant pot and add in coconut milk and coconut cream. Lock lid and cook on high for 10 Mins and then let pressure come down on its own.
4. Meanwhile, whisk together the dressing ingredients and set aside.
5. Combine together the salad ingredients in a mixing bowl.
6. Serve the fish with coconut sauce on plates and top each with the salad. Enjoy!

Nutrition : Calories: 341; Total Fat: 11.6 g; Carbs: 11 g; Dietary Fiber: 2.1 g; Sugars: 4.1 g; Protein: 21 g; Cholesterol: 0 mg; Sodium: 245 mg

Tilapia with Mushroom Sauce

Yields: 4 | Total Time: 45 Mins | Prep Time: 15 Mins | Cook Time: 30 Mins

Ingredients

- 6 ounces tilapia fillets
- 2 teaspoon arrowroot
- 1 cup mushrooms, sliced
- 1 clove garlic, finely chopped
- 1 small onion, thinly sliced
- 2 tablespoons extra virgin olive oil
- ½ cup fresh parsley, roughly chopped
- 1 teaspoon thyme leaves, finely chopped
- ½ cup water
- A pinch of freshly ground black pepper
- A pinch of sea salt

Directions

1. Add extra virgin olive oil to an instant pot and set on manual high; sauté onion, garlic and mushrooms for about 4 Mins or until mushrooms are slightly tender.
2. Stir in arrowroot, sea salt, thyme and pepper and cook for about 1 minute.
3. Stir in water until thickened; stir in parsley and cook for 1 minute more.
4. Place the fillets in the pot and cover with mushroom sauce, lock lid and cook on high for 20 Mins. Let pressure come down on its own.

Nutrition : Calories: 177; Total Fat: 7.2 g; Carbs: 3.3 g; Dietary Fiber: 1.4 g; Sugars: 1.1 g; Protein: 14.9 g; Cholesterol: 1 mg; Sodium: 66 mg

Pressure Cooked Salmon with Herbs

Yield: 4 | Total Time: 21 Mins | Prep Time: 15 Mins | Cook Time: 6 Mins

Ingredients

- 8 ounces wild salmon fillets
- Fennel fronds
- 1 tablespoon chopped parsley
- 1 tablespoon chopped dill
- 1 tablespoon chopped chives
- 1 tablespoon chopped tarragon
- 1 tablespoon chopped basil
- 1 tablespoon extra virgin olive oil
- 1 tablespoon chopped shallot
- 1 tablespoon lemon juice

Directions

1. Lightly oil a steamer basket with olive oil; add salmon and fennel wedges. Add water to an instant pot and insert a metal trivet; place the steamer over the trivet and cook for 6 Mins.
2. In a bowl, combine the chopped herbs, extra virgin olive oil, shallot and lemon juice; stir until well combined. Season and spoon over cooked fish.

Nutrition : Calories: 98; Total Fat: 6.3 g; Carbs: 2.5 g; Dietary Fiber: 0.9 g; sugars: trace; Protein: 8.9 g; Cholesterol: 19 mg; Sodium: 33 mg

Instant Pot White Fish Curry

Yield: 2 | Total Time: 30 Mins | Prep Time: 10 Mins | Cook Time: 20 Mins

Ingredients

- 2 tablespoons olive oil
- 200g white fish filet, diced
- ¼ cup fish broth
- Pinch of turmeric
- Dash of onion powder
- 1 tablespoon minced red onion
- Pinch of garlic powder
- ¼ teaspoon curry powder
- Pinch of sea salt
- Pinch of pepper
- Stevia

Directions

1. Set an instant pot on sauté mode, heat oil and sauté onion and garlic; stir in fish filet and cook until browned. Stir spices in fish broth and Stevia and add to the pot. Lock lid and cook on high for 15 Mins. Release the pressure naturally and serve hot over steamed veggies.

Nutrition : Calories: 213; Fat: 17.4g; Carbs: 2.3g; Protein: 20.5g

Pressure Roasted Tilapia

Yield: 6 | Total Time: 1 Hour 40 Mins | Prep Time: 10 Mins | Cook Time: 1 Hour 30 Mins

Ingredients:

- 4 tablespoons extra virgin olive oil
- ½ cup apple cider vinegar
- 3 cloves garlic, minced
- 2-3 tablespoons minced ginger
- 2 pounds Tilapia Fillets
- 1-pound chopped carrots
- handful of rosemary
- Pinch of sea salt
- Pinch of pepper

Directions:

1. Place Tilapia in aluminum foil. In a bowl, whisk together olive oil, apple cider vinegar, garlic, and ginger until well combined; pour over the fish and top with carrots and rosemary. Sprinkle with salt and pepper and fold to wrap well. Add water to an instant pot and insert a metal trivet. Place the foil over the trivet and cook on high for 1 ½ hours. Let pressure come down naturally.

Nutrition : Calories: 331; Total Fat: 18.7 g; Carbs: 6.3 g; Dietary Fiber: 1.8 g; Sugars: 2.5 g; Protein: 37.4 g; Cholesterol: 122 mg; Sodium: 225 mg

Instant Pot Roasted Salmon

Yield: 6 | Total Time: 1 Hour 40 Mins | Prep Time: 10 Mins | Cook Time: 1Hour 30 Mins

Ingredients:

- 1 tablespoon extra virgin olive oil
- ½ cup apple cider vinegar
- 3 cloves garlic, minced
- 2-3 tablespoons minced ginger
- 2 pounds salmon fillets
- 1 pound chopped carrots
- handful of rosemary
- Pinch of sea salt
- Pinch of pepper

Directions

1. Place salmon in your instant pot. In a bowl, whisk together olive oil, apple cider vinegar, garlic, and ginger until well combined; pour over the fish and top with carrots and rosemary. Sprinkle with salt and pepper and lock lid. Cook on high setting for 1 ½ hours and then let pressure come down on its own. Serve warm over steamed veggies.

Nutrition : Calories: 372; Total Fat: 14.6 g; Carbs: 7.6 g; Dietary Fiber: 1.7 g; Sugars: 3.3 g; Protein: 50 g; Cholesterol: 151 mg; Sodium: 220 mg

Instant Pot Tilapia in Coconut Cream Sauce

Yields: 2 | Total Time: 25 Mins | Prep Time: 5 Mins | Cook Time: 20 Mins

Ingredients

- 2 tablespoons olive oil
- 2 tilapia filets
- 2 red onions
- 2 minced cloves garlic
- 1 medium red bell pepper, diced
- 1/4 cup low-sodium soy sauce
- 1/4 tsp. crushed red pepper flakes
- ¼ cup coconut cream

Directions

1. Set your instant pot on sauté mode and heat olive oil; sauté the red onion and garlic until fragrant and then cook tilapia filets until browned on both sides. Stir in the remaining ingredients and lock lid; cook on high setting for 10 Mins. Quick release the pressure and serve.

Nutrition : Calories: 262; Total Fat: 8.6 g; Carbs: 11.1g; Dietary Fiber: 1.4 g; Sugars: 7.7 g; Protein: 34.8 g; Cholesterol: 101 mg; Sodium: 1170 mg

Made in the USA
Coppell, TX
03 January 2020

14039300R00085